Metal

designs
material
technique

John Hack

VNR VAN NOSTRAND REINHOLD COMPANY
New York Cincinnati Toronto London Melbourne

This book was originally
published in German under the
title *Metallarbeiten* by Otto
Maier Verlag, Ravensburg,
Germany

Copyright © Otto Maier Verlag,
Ravensburg, 1970
English translation © Van
Nostrand Reinhold Company
Ltd. 1972

Library of Congress Catalog
Card Number 70-183493
ISBN 0442 03005 3 cl.
0442 03005 1 pb.

Jewellery designs:
Alexander Calder page 81—85
Ruth Koblassa page 35
Paula Strauss page 29—30

This book is set in Univers and is
printed in Great Britain by
Jolly and Barber Ltd., Rugby
and bound by Richard Clay
(The Chaucer Press Ltd.)
Bungay, Suffolk

Published by Van Nostrand
Reinhold Company, Inc.
450 West 33rd St., New York,
N.Y. 10001 and Van Nostrand
Reinhold Company Ltd.
Windsor House, 46 Victoria
Street, London S.W.1

Published simultaneously in
Canada by Van Nostrand
Reinhold Company Ltd.

16   15   14   13   12   11   10   9   8   7   6   5   4   3   2   1

Contents

Starting right   5

The Materials   7

Gold   7
Silver   8
Copper   8
Brass and nickel silver   9

Treatment   10

The Tools   12

Silver Jewellery   13

Necklace in silver wire   13
Necklace with regular spirals   15
Woven link necklace or bracelet   15
Bead and spiral necklace   18
Necklace of semi-precious stones   20
Domed disc necklace   21
Stirrup pattern necklace   23
Beaten double-ring chain   26
Double-oval ring chain   28
Silver necklace with domes and stone   29
A delightful variation   30
Meander-pattern brooch   31
Ear-ring   33
Ring and cross necklace   34
Silver chain with flat wire rings   35
Long dome necklace   36
Ring with cone-shaped stone   38
Drilled stone ring   40

Gold Jewellery with Wire and Sheet   41

Gold chain-mail necklace with pearls   41
Gold ring with pearl   43

Wire and Sheet Brass for Bigger Items   45

Pretzel stand   45
A similar stand for table napkins   47
Another stand — wire and sheet metal   50
Three or four armed candlestick   52
Paper-knife from sheet metal — sawn and filed   57
Fondue fork   58
Container for cigarettes, tea or coffee   60
Salad-servers   62
Coat rack and umbrella stand   64
Hall-light with variations   66
Hall-light with sheet brass reflector   68

Hollowing and Raising   70

Decorative Processes   75

Punching and inscribing   75
Ancient and modern American jewellery   80
Rifflers   86
Needle or Swiss files   87

Index   88

Starting right

To watch, for example, an Arabian metalworker hammering and soldering wire and sheet metal is to be impressed above all with the gentle playfulness of the activity. Crouched in the shadow of his doorway, using knee and thigh as an anvil, with only nails for punches and a rough, rudimentary kind of hammer, he transforms a sheet of copper or brass into a succession of shapes that swell finally into the beauty of a bowl. Very little has changed since the time of the Pharaohs, it seems, and our modern Arab could well be a replica of one of the smiths portrayed on an ancient Egyptian fresco.

Such skill, unaided by anything except the bare minimum of tools, is cause not only for wonder and admiration but also for the conviction that improvisation is often the best source of what is novel and original.

But why, you may ask, this emphasis on the primitive right at the beginning? There is no other reason than the experience of pure joy accompanying our first attempts to create something for ourselves. Satisfaction comes not so much from a technical fluency as from the urge to continue which is aroused even by the most unsuccessful of efforts. The satisfaction is so much greater when the first steps forward are made in conditions quite different from those to be found in a modern well equipped workshop.

Take for example the youth with an apparently strong inclination towards a particular hobby who amasses a small collection of tools, among which a bench vice, hammers, saws, files and so on come in for individual care and admiration, until gradually it becomes apparent that in this case the joy is one of acquisition rather than craftsmanship. When the youth recognizes this fact it is no great sacrifice to give up his workshop.

The opposite is true in the case of prisoners of war, who without either workshop or tools had created the domestic necessities of life from the mass of tin cans and boxes around them. Here these inexperienced amateurs felt compelled to produce cups and plates, cases and utensils of all kinds from this versatile tin plate. Very often it is the complete stranger to the craft who develops most skill because he has to find out for himself — literally with no more than a stone and a few nails — how to construct a joint, attach a base or finish an edge.

But what is the significance of all this for our introduction to making things out of metal? Simply this, that there are many ways of arriving at the goal, and discovery and invention, both in the technical and artistic sense, are things that the enthusiastic craftsman will experience for himself as he tries to give visible form to the promptings of his imagination.

Metal is not, however, the best material to put into the hands of the would-be craftsman, unlike clay or plaster where errors need leave no mark and the material by its very nature can be thrown together again for a completely fresh start. There is little room for error with metal, and occasionally there is the disappointment of spoiling a piece of work and having to discard it completely.

For this reason, as well as another dealt with in the conclusion, the beginner should be given an introduction to the craft of metalwork. By introducing a few carefully selected examples appropriate to his slowly developing skills, this book aims to indicate the most practical approach to the job while avoiding the exhaustion and disappointment accompanying the trial and error approach. In this way, it is hoped that the beginner will learn enough to develop the skill and self-confidence needed to make more advanced attempts.

The one-sided technical specialization of modern times needs the counterbalancing influence of the amateur's leisure-time handicraft. The more people make things for themselves with their own hands, the sooner will a critical sense be developed preventing the indiscriminate purchase of the ugly and useless among mass produced goods, and promoting instead a demand for products which are both useful and attractive.

However, discrimination and judgement are more difficult to develop than the techniques of soldering and hammering, and it is possible for the benefits of craftsmanship to be squandered by a wild wave of enthusiastic but indiscriminate production of enough brooches, clasps and headbands to adorn every woman in sight in a deluge of brass jewellery. Nothing is more likely to lower standards and to reduce the handicraft than absurdity.

This is the second reason for undertaking this short introduction: a plea not to copy the production of the rather useless knick-knacks which can be purchased in so many novelty stores, such as imitation antique ashtrays, or extravagantly styled imitation Renaissance lanterns. Why waste time on such things when even in the souvenir shops of the crowded tourist resorts they are regarded as just so much trash.

Our efforts should reward us not only with a few days of delight but with years of pleasure. It is therefore important to consider the form of the finished object as well as the technique of production. Ultimately it is a matter of a revolution of standards. The hobby begins as a focus of discontentment with the ordinary and from that grows into a critical desire for the improvement of our environment. In this way we can avoid the rather fruitless discussions about the endlessly intriguing term "Taste", and instead get down to the practical production of objects which either please or displease in function and appearance. Indeed, one hammer blow is sufficient to dispose of the unsatisfactory. There is much more pleasure to be gained from making one's own objects than in constant criticism of the works of others.

That is really all that needs to be said about starting the craft in the right way. Given the right attitude, the relevant technical questions will follow, and they are dealt with in the rest of the book. One request though: the author of a book like this seldom knows whether or not his hopes are realized in the efforts of the beginner he would like to inspire. For this reason the publisher will be happy to receive photographs of things made as a result of reading this book.

The Materials

Gold

In the U.K. permission is required from H.M. Treasury to buy gold under the Exchange Control Act, 1947. In the USA gold may be purchased in small quantities from private industry such as smelters. However, because of its price, it is unlikely to play a significant role in metalwork as a hobby. Just the same, we should mention some of its most important characteristics both for general information and more especially for the few who may be enticed into using it.

It is available in three basic forms; sheet, wire and granules. The colour varies from yellow to red, depending on the composition of the alloy. Usual standards: fine gold = 1000/1000; 18 carat gold = 750/1000; 14 carat gold = 585/1000; 9 carat gold = 375/1000. In other words, 24 carat gold is fine gold with a rating of 1000/1000. As the most malleable of all metals, gold might be regarded as the ideal material for the amateur, but fine gold (although there are some who do excellent work with it) is generally too soft for most people. Gold wire is easily drawn and bent into shape, while thin gold sheet can be worked even with wooden modelling tools. For information about soldering this metal, however, you will have to look elsewhere since the size of this short introduction makes it impossible to deal adequately with it.

Silver

It is safe to assume that there are one or two who will want to work in silver, at least on the smaller pieces of jewellery where the cost is of no great significance. A strip of sheet-silver can be used to make a paper-knife or an attractive spoon at a relatively low cost.

Fine silver is too soft for most work. For that reason it is available in alloy form in various standards. In England, for example, it is available as 925/1000 and 958·4/1000, the first figures indicate how many parts of silver per thousand are mixed with copper and zinc to make up the alloy. The English term "sterling" has been in use since 1300 A.D. to indicate a composition of 925/1000.

Silver is also available as wire and sheet, the latter being designated by tenths of a millimetre.

Annealing is necessary to counter the work-hardening that occurs as a result of hammering silver into shape. The silver is heated, preferably in a darkened room, until a blush of red appears. After cooling and before further working, the resulting oxidized layer must be removed (see "Pickling", page 10).

Silver solder should have a high silver content and a low melting point (from 600°–900°C) and is obtainable as sheet, wire or filings. Solder with a 48–50 per cent silver content flows relatively easily. Hard solder containing 64–68 per cent silver has a higher melting point. The use of silver solder is not confined to silver objects but plays a significant role in all metalwork. Brass boxes, for example, are much better soldered with soft silver solder than with tin, and the joint is more attractive and durable.

Copper

This attractive, soft metal, with its range of multicoloured variations, has unfortunately been rediscovered by enterprising "folk-artists" who have used it to make rather unattractive flower tubs, heating trays and so on, to meet the demands of the "modern" householder.

I prefer the more simple things in which a combination of size and solidity show up the red-coloured metal at its best.

But first here are one or two details about the character of this metal. Soldering is not the best thing for copper because of the adverse effect the heat has on the richness of the colour. Joints are therefore better seamed or riveted.

A coating of Japan lacquer preserves the light red colour of the copper. Otherwise exposure to the air leads to the formation of a chestnut-brown patina on the surface, an effect which is by no means unattractive, and which is in some cases to be desired. Various chemicals can be used for permanently colouring the copper, sulphur compounds, such as potassium sulphide and sodium sulphide produce effects ranging from brown to black tints. Copper chloride produces bronze to green tints. Brown to red tints are produced with acid compounds.

For successful colouring of copper the surface must be clean and free of oxide, dirt or grease. De-grease with damp French chalk, wash off with water, clean up with a brass or steel wire-brush. Apply the solution thinly and evenly with a brush or cloth, rub in and leave to dry before applying the next coating of the solution. The most attractive and durable results are obtained by applying a number of coats and rubbing each one thoroughly with a soft piece of cloth or leather. If weaker solutions are applied and treated in this way, a polished finish is obtained which reflects the natural patina of the copper.

For colouring, a solution of Schlipper's Salt, applied warm or cold, produces a tone ranging between yellowish-brown and dark brown, depending on the strength of the solution and the duration of the treatment. For a reddish-brown-copper tone use a solution of two parts verdigris, two parts cinnabar, five parts sal-ammoniac, five parts alum and vinegar.

Brass and nickel silver

One of the alloys most suitable for metalwork is brass, an alloy of copper and zinc. It is available in sheet, tube and wire form, both half-hard and soft temper. The soft brass is easiest to use. It is once again in fashion for bowls, light units, boxes and flower-pot stands. The metal shows up best with a matt finish.

The alloy coding indicates the percentage of copper in the brass. For our purpose standard brass with a 63 per cent copper content is best. In addition, Dutch metal (80 per cent copper), Malay brass or Tombac (85 per cent copper) and red brass (90 per cent copper) can be worked cold as well. Enamelling brass should not contain more than 8 per cent zinc.

Nickel silver is an alloy composed of copper, zinc and nickel, the latter producing both the hardness and the yellowish-white colour which make nickel silver unsuitable for our kind of work. Though it is quite well suited to industrial production, the metal does, however, present problems to the amateur. He will be disappointed to find that, from the beginning, his treatment of the metal will produce a most unattractive surface.

Treatment

Pumice-stone is excellent for smoothing metal, especially silver. Used with water both the solid stone and the powder produce a first-class finish. Rotten stone, aluminium oxide, French chalk and whiting are finer and tend to polish the material — something that is rarely needed. French chalk can be obtained as a paste in tube form.

Emery-cloth and emery-paper are available in various grades from rough to smooth. Wrapped around a lath or an old file, flat or half round, to ensure proper contact with the surface, to be finished, emery-paper should be worked first in different directions, and then finally in one direction only, along the length of the object, in order to produce the best finish.

Soldering can be done only if the surface of the metal is clean. A scraper, file or emery-cloth can be used to clean the joint before applying the flux to preserve cleanliness during the soldering process.

Solders are obtainable in solid or liquid form. For soft soldering (with tin) a flux can be made up of 27 parts chlorate of zinc, 11 parts sal-ammoniac, 62 parts water. Core solder is extremely practical as it is made up of a tin solder tube with a core of zinc-chloride flux. In addition fluxes are obtainable in powder and paste form.

Hard soldering, using silver solder, can be done in a number of ways: stick soldering with a paste flux; strip soldering with a specially prepared powdered flux or Borax, or panel soldering, in which the solder is cut into small chips and laid along the joint with Borax.

To make a paste: The Borax is made into a paste by rubbing it with a circular motion in its cone form in a Borax tray, into which a few drops of water have been placed. It is used in powdered form when soldering large joints. Sometimes at about 400°C, the Borax flux may bubble and prevent the solder taking. (In such cases another kind of flux may be used.) At temperatures over 700°C, however, the salt melts and its glassy consistency effectively seals the joint and thus prevents oxidization. This film can be removed later by pickling in a hot acid solution, which consists of dilute sulphuric acid — one part of acid to ten parts of water.

As well as being used to remove the Borax, pickling also follows the annealing and soldering operations to bring about the removal of the oxides and impurities which have formed on the surface of the metal. The pickle can also be used for cleaning the brass, copper and silver objects. A serious warning must be given on the necessity for caution in handling concentrated sulphuric acid. Water must never be poured into the acid as the immediate vaporizing of the water will cause the acid to split explosively in all directions. In order to prevent any accidents, pour the acid slowly into the water, stirring lightly at the same time with a piece of wood. Avoid getting splashes of the solution on your clothes, otherwise the next wash-day will reveal a number of holes. The pickle is best stored in a stoneware pot which can be covered with a sheet of glass when not in use. A strip of wood or length of aluminium wire should be used to handle the materials that are placed in the pickle bath.

The same pickling solution can be used for blanching silver. First bring the pickle to the boil before immersing the object, and leave for about five or ten minutes, before removing the object and drying with a cloth. Repeat this process three or four times, annealing again between immersions if necessary. After each pickling, brush vigorously with a brass wire-brush, and after the final pickling leave to dry in a container of warmed sawdust. The purpose of this whole operation is to remove the copper element of the alloy from the surface of the metal and to reveal the fine silver layer beneath.

"Repoussé" is the technical term used to include the techniques of chasing and embossing illustrated by figures 30, 32 and 33. You can either make the tools or buy a kit of tools quite cheaply.

A good recipe for the pitch underlayer used in this particular process is 4 lb. Swedish pitch, 6 lb. plaster of Paris or brick dust, a little tallow and some turpentine to soften the mixture. (The latter can be omitted if you want to work on a rather harder surface.) Warm, stir the mixture and leave to dry. Naturally it must be warmed each time before use.

The Tools

To make the things described in this book, you will need only a few tools, and they can be bought quite cheaply. Nearly all the tools mentioned are available in ordinary hardware stores, or they can be ordered by mail from large craft suppliers whose catalogues indicate the wide range of tools they stock. You will need a general purpose hammer (with a head weighing about 8 oz. and an ash-wood handle), planishing and chasing hammers, and a mallet. An anvil, with a 3 in. face, and stakes of various kinds (with either a stake horse or a hardwood block to hold them) are also necessary.

In addition files of different sections and cuts will be needed as well as tin-shears, soldering-iron and core solder as previously mentioned. To start with, instead of an expensive electric soldering-iron, it may be better to buy a soldering kit containing iron, blow-torch, soldering wire and sal-ammoniac stone.

Do not overlook, as you equip your workshop, the satisfaction you would get from making and using tools of your own design, which in fact turn out to be more suitable for your purpose than an elaborately equipped workshop.

Silver Jewellery

Necklace in silver wire

The beginner can make a start with an attractive piece of jewellery whose charm comes from its apparent imperfection — the slight difference between one square spiral and the next, as you can see from the photograph. This is no different in fact from the primitive charm of necklaces of teeth, blossoms or clay beads in which the irregularity of the separate units lends vitality to the overall design.

The materials needed are a three feet length of 1 mm. thick silver wire, a pair of pliers for cutting the wire, and round-nosed pliers, as illustrated for bending the wire. A rough sketch on paper or cardboard determines the outline and the dimensions and also provides a template to follow when bending the wire.

With the round-nose pliers hold one end of cut wire over the middle point of the sketch and bend the spiral into shape from the centre point outwards, following the lines of the sketch. Finally, the triangular-shaped eye is formed by bending the end of the wire to the right or left as shown in

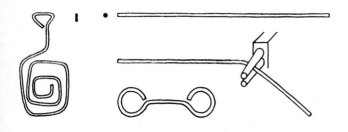

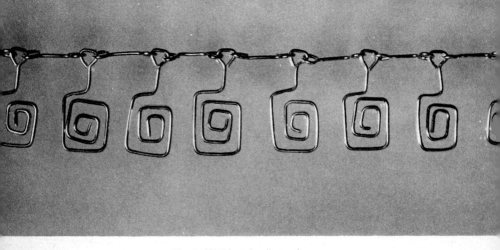

Fig. 1. Necklace in silver wire.

the photograph. The eyes should not be formed, however, before completing all the spiral shapes first and then placing them side by side before cutting off any excess from the neck in order to ensure that they are the same size. The next step is to make the simple links shown in the sketch.

The size of these links can be gauged by placing the spiral shapes in a row and moving them until you find the best distance between them; then cut off a length of wire, allowing for the loops as well as for the distance between the spirals, bend into shape and place between a pair of the spirals to ensure that it stands properly in relation both to the spirals and to the size and pattern of the whole necklace. When satisfied, you can make the rest of the links.

To join the spirals to the intermediate links all that remains is to decide which eyes shall be closed completely and which left slightly open for looping later through the enclosed ones. Whichever way is chosen an attractive necklace can be made without the complication of soldering, thus beginning your metalworking career with a piece of jewellery which is simple, uncomplicated and pleasing to the eye.

14

Fig. 2. Necklace with regular spirals.

Necklace with regular spirals

This is a slight variation of the first necklace which again avoids soldering. The only difference is that the open, square spiral becomes a regular, more tightly wound spiral as you can see in the photograph. Note also the way in which the spirals are hung so that the element of counterpoint is introduced to give a feeling of rhythm to the necklace. Use the round-nose pliers for bending the wire into spiral shapes in the same way as before or, even better, a strong wire with an eye at one end (like a sardine can opener). The end of the silver wire is inserted into the slit and then rotated to produce a fairly lightly coiled spiral. The connecting links are made in the same way as for the last necklace.

Woven link necklace or bracelet

The next exercise involves soldering. In addition to the two pairs of pliers used in the previous exercises, we need soft silver solder and Borax or a patented flux. Although the fantastically skilful craftsmen of ancient times used no more than charcoal and a blowpipe, it is better to use a gas tube attachment (if there is gas available) or a Bunsen-burner and blowpipe to direct the flame onto the work. In any case, for soldering wire only a small flame is necessary, and a home-made blowpipe is good enough.

To make individual loops for the necklace or bracelet

Fig. 3. Woven link necklace or bracelet. Additional tools: flat-nosed pliers for stretching binding wire, blowpipe, bow-saw and appropriate saw blades.

16

shown in the photograph, the technique illustrated in the sketch is used. As shown, use a wooden rod to wind a regular coiled spring, out of soft silver, copper or brass wire, or, if anodising facilities are available, out of aluminium wire which can be most attractively dyed afterwards in a variety of colours. The coils of the spring should be wound closely together, for a distance of about 2 in. along the rod.

After the removal from the rod, the spring is held together with binding wire so that it can be sawn in one operation to produce the single coils needed to make the folded loops of the necklace or the bracelet.

The first thing to do after separating the coils is to bring the ends of each loop into line and closer together. Sawing leaves the ends of the wire in their pure metallic state which is ideal for soldering. Before soldering, the ends of the loops must have been bent just that much past each other to close the circle completely when they are left free to spring back.

Soldering is not half as difficult as the layman assumes. In fact, an increasing number of young sculptors decorate their metal sculpture with the very things that a master-solderer would regard as faults. For example, too hot a flame wrinkles the surface of the metal. A technical fault like this is used by an enterprising metal sculptor to produce strange and intriguing effects. However, beginners should learn the correct way to solder.

For the working surface, fix an asbestos sheet to a piece of sheet metal with strong adhesive. Use wire mesh if soldering is done with a Bunsen-burner.

Solder, 4 mm. thick, can be bought in sheets or panels, cut first into narrow strips and then into $\frac{1}{2}$ mm. chips. A single chip is enough to solder the ends of the loops together without having to file off unsightly lumps of solder afterwards. If more solder is necessary, it may be that the loop ends have sprung open too far. More solder will further enlarge the loop with a resulting lack of symmetry in the whole necklace.

Patented fluxes are available in hardware stores and they not only prevent oxidization but also hold the chip of the solder in the joint. They are often better than a Borax flux, which can bubble up and move the solder chip out of position.

Liquid or paste fluxes can be applied with a fine brush to the joint to be soldered and the brush can then be used to transfer the solder chip to the joint. The flame is carefully played on the joint until the chip of solder gently swells like a drop of water before closing the joint.

After all the loops have been soldered each one is pinched into a figure-of-eight shape, as shown in the sketch. The best way to do this is to stick two dowels or strong pencils at opposite ends inside the loop, and then to pinch the wire together, first with the fingers and finally with small round-

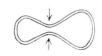

nose pliers. The next step of the operation consists of folding the double loop to resemble a clothing-hook, as shown in the sketch, and here too use a small wooden dowel or the end of a fountain-pen to preserve the shape of the loops. Before completely closing the fold of the loop the next folded loop is inserted in position. Attached in this way, there is a danger of the links working loose from the necklace or bracelet, and to prevent this, each link is spot-soldered where the overlapping loops meet.

Bead and spiral necklace

Here is a necklace that can be copied exactly as illustrated in the photograph, or made in a slightly different style. It is one of the best examples of making an almost unlimited number of attractive variations from a single basic pattern. For that reason detailed working instructions are unnecessary.

Although the necklace in the photograph has six strands, you can include more or less as you wish. The choice of colours is open since glass beads come in every colour. The original is composed of dull white, imitation pearls, with translucent green and rose quartz-like beads, interspersed with coral red pearls. With the accent on green and coral red, it is a colourful, eye-catching necklace.

Similarly the wire links can be varied. There is no complete regularity either in shape or arrangement, and the necklace lacks any strict symmetry. The eye sees harmony in the whole as it flashes from segment to segment and is intrigued by a riot of colour and form that combine in a kaleidoscopic effect.

A further explanation of the way in which the wire is threaded through the beads before the ends are looped into eyelets is unnecessary. There is no need either to explain again how to make the spring-like connecting links by winding lengths of wire around a strip of thin rod. This is a necklace that can be made without the necessity of soldering, although in our example the eyelets at the ends of the bead threading wire mentioned above, were soldered for extra strength. It would be enough to bend them with a pair of pliers. In fact, the necklace is a creation that makes no technical demands upon the amateur, and its flexibility of form allows incidental problems to be solved or side-stepped as they arise.

The clasp consists of a triangular shaped hook and eye large enough to take the strands of the necklace. At this point, the strength of each strand's connecting eyelet could be improved by soldering.

Fig. 4. Bead and spiral necklace.
Materials: brass wire, later gold-plated. Glass beads in various colours.

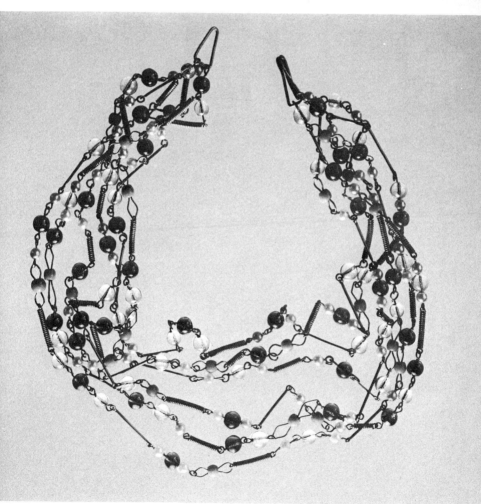

Necklace of semi-precious stones

The success of the attractive necklace shown in the photograph is the result of a well developed artistic sense. Its construction presents no technical problems. All that is required is the ability to select the right variety of semi-precious stones and to arrange them harmoniously together, using links and fastenings that are bought rather than made by the beginner.

Fig. 5. Necklace of semi-precious stones in a variety of colours.

Unfortunately the black and white photograph conveys very little of the colourful variety of the stones. Amethysts, rose quartz and smoky quartz stones are juxtaposed in a succession of blending colours and contrasts of dark and light, with violet following pink, and brilliance fading, as the smoky colour of the quartz mingles between one stone and another. The irregularity of the stones contributes to the shimmer of colour. They are unfaceted, irregular stones which can be bought from lapidary suppliers.

Buy stones with the holes already bored. The thin gold chain (0·8 mm. thick) and the small gold beads (2–2$\frac{1}{2}$ mm. diameter) strung between the stones can be obtained from hobby shops. As a rule the beads will have to be drilled right through, since the blind hole which is usual pierces only one face of the casing. It is possible, however, to buy gold beads that are drilled right through

After threading the chain through the stones and beads, the last step is to attach the rod and the ring that make up the clasp of the necklace. The ring is soldered onto a small gold bead fixed to the end of the gold chain, while the rod is soldered onto a ring which is loosely attached by a smaller eyelet also soldered onto the gold bead at the other end of the chain.

Domed disc necklace

The small domed discs shown as part of the necklace in the photograph on the next page start off as flat silver discs which are given their shape by means of the doming block illustrated in the lower left hand sketch, and the doming tool above the disc (in section) in the right hand sketch. The steel doming block has a number of regular concavities into which the discs are punched to make domes. Wooden hollowing blocks can also be made from elm, beech or even ebony, the hollows being gouged out. Punches can be bought in sets or even made at home. For doming soft metal like thin (0·4–0·5 mm.) silver discs, even wooden punches may be used. The process simply consists of placing the disc over the hollow in the block and then depressing it with a doming punch. Instead of a wooden or steel doming block, a thick lead sheet may be used. The ball punch is hammered lightly into the lead, and the resulting depression is used for the doming operation already described.

The sketch shows the domes full size, although there is no need to stick slavishly to these dimensions. The domes are drilled with two holes as shown, and linked together by means of short lengths of wire bent over at the ends as shown in the sketch below. A refinement in the linkage, which would also make a more flexible necklace, is a blob of solder at each end of the wire, instead of bending as shown in the sketch.

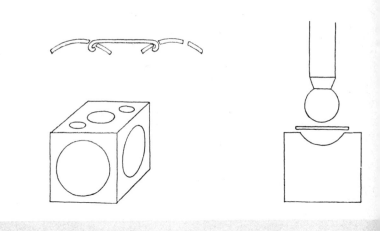

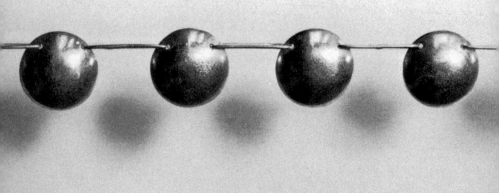

Fig. 6. Domed disc necklace.

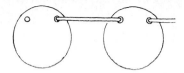

Stirrup pattern necklace

In addition to wire, for the first time a small piece of sheet silver (925/1000, 0·6 mm. thick) is needed. Naturally sheet brass can be used instead but in the case of such small amounts of metal being involved, there is really no appreciable difference in price — and brass jewellery is not very attractive. Silver plating afterwards is a rather costly and elaborate process, and even so it is unlikely to match the charm of genuine silver.

800/1000 silver is also unsuitable for jewellery because it tarnishes with wearing, for this reason sterling silver is preferable.

Make a working sketch on heavy drawing paper of the U-shaped silver unit in its flat state. Cutting out and bending into shape helps to produce a sketch of the right proportions. Transfer the final sketch onto stout card for use as a template. The surface of the silver is coated with gamboge. Then mark the outline of the template on it in such a way that the units can be cut out with the minimum of waste. The separate pieces are then cut out either with a saw or

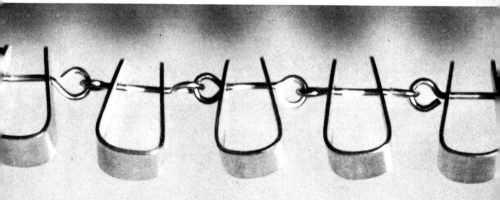

Fig. 7. Stirrup pattern necklace made out of wire and sheet metal. For sawing, a compass saw or small hack-saw, with suitable blades.

23

with tin-snips. The resulting burr on the edges will have to be filed flat.

After filing the edges flat, the next step is to drill the holes in the ends as shown in the sketch (page 23). When the pieces are bent into the stirrup shape, the holes will take the twin looped wire links, as shown in the photograph.

All that is needed for drilling is the conventional hand drill and bits made from pieces of steel wire, flattened and filed into shape and then hardened and tempered. Unlike the usual drill bits, they can cut clockwise or anti-clockwise.

The ribs of an old umbrella make good flat bits. Cut off a length of rib, heat in a flame and beat flat. Then anneal and file into shape as shown in the sketch on page 25. Finally, heat to a cherry red colour, plunge into water, thus bringing the bit to a glass hard state before sharpening ready for use.

With such a bit, equivalent in diameter to the size of the wire, drill the holes in the individual sheet silver units. Any burr that forms may be removed by using a slightly larger bit and turning it very lightly once over the hole.

With a suitable piece of dowelling, the silver strip can now be bent into its finished stirrup shape. Use a pair of pliers to hold the wooden rod and silver strip together and fingers to do the bending. Check with the sketch to ensure regularity and symmetry. Finally, lay out the stirrups in a row to determine the size of the silver wire links, bearing in mind not only the distance between the silver stirrups but also the loops at each end of the link.

At first only one end of the wire link is looped. The second one is formed only after the wire has been pushed through the stirrup. Then follow these operations:

Wire links are cut to length; each one is looped at one end only before sticking the straight end through the drill holes in the stirrup. Finally, the formation of the second loop joins them together.

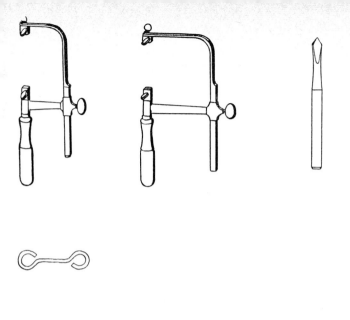

Fig. 8. Chain — not described in the text — but easy to make.

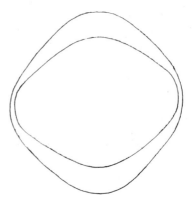

Beaten double-ring chain

With the technical tricks of the trade mastered during the previous exercises, you can now undertake a variety of projects. The chain shown in the left hand photograph on the opposite page consists basically of loops made (as previously described on pages 15–18) by spiralling, sawing and soldering the ends of the rings. At opposite ends of the diameter, where the two rings touch and where they are drilled to take the connecting links, they are beaten wider, as shown in the sketch, before bending each ring at right angles, as can be seen in the photograph.

The figure-of-eight connecting links are made from thin wire, and they can either be closed with a pair of pliers after passing through the drill holes or, for extra strength and technical finesse, soldered where the horizontal rings touch. The effect of an open sphere is increased by the movement of the bent rings: pulling away at the perimeter and angled to keep contact in the middle.

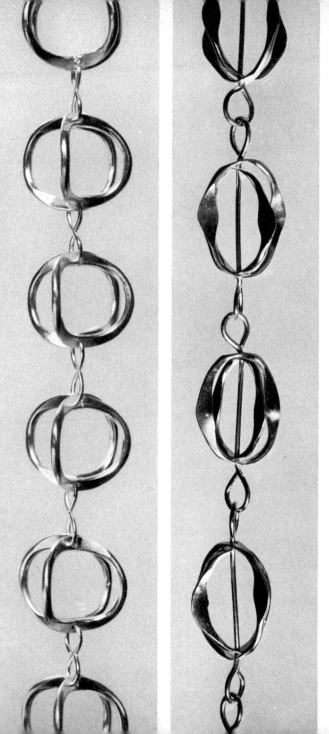

Fig. 9. Beaten double-ring chain. Tools as before. Wire in two thicknesses: 1 mm. for the double-rings and 0·5 mm. for the figure of eight links.

Fig. 10. (near right) A variation: double-oval ring chain. A different shape, with through-links.

Double-oval ring chain

The chain shown in the right-hand photograph on page 27, is made in much the same way. It is a closely related variation of its neighbour. This is to remind you that this book is intended to be much more than just an instruction manual with examples that must be slavishly copied. It is meant to stimulate you to produce things creatively. Many striking and original forms lie waiting to be discovered.

The essential difference between this chain and the last is that this one consists of two different sized rings so that one can fit inside the other as shown in the photograph. Now oval instead of round, the rings are joined by links of wire passing through the middle, as shown in the sketch.

The rings are spread differently as well. There is a slight spreading where the holes are to be drilled but it is much more pronounced on both sides of each of the interlocking rings, as shown in the sketch below. In this way, the otherwise sculptured stiffness of plain rings is transformed into an ovoid shape which is both open and primitive in appearance. The attractive connecting links are cut and looped as described previously.

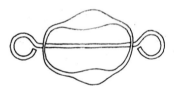

Silver necklace with domes and stone

This cheap little necklace, intended for a young girl, is so simple that no one would suspect it of being the work of a rather well-known goldsmith, quickly and attractively produced for a special occasion.

The chain is bought ready-made. The discs are domed as already described, and the rose quartz stone is bought with a hole drilled through. The stone shown in the photograph is by no means perfect but its imperfections hardly detract from the attractive design of the necklace. Mounting the silver discs and the stone is no problem. A silver chain is pushed through the hole in the stone and provided with double twisted eyelets close to the stone at each end. The discs are mounted on S-shaped pieces of wire, provided with loops at each end, one to be linked to the double eyelet of the wire holding the stone and the other to the chain. The clasp, too, is simplicity itself: a silver wire bent into the shape of a hook is looped firmly over one end of the chain with the aid of a pair of pliers. The eye for the hook consists simply of the link at the other end of the chain.

Fig. 11. Silver chain with rose quartz stone and domed silver discs.

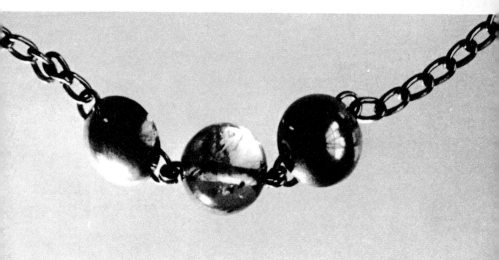

A delightful variation

The charming necklace illustrated below, made for a child, is the work of the same goldsmith, and the style and composition clearly show the influences of her art school days. It consists of a ready-made silver chain with a conventional spring clasp, to set off an essentially simple and youthful arrangement of round stones of clear quartz, green flecked agate together with five red coral chips. What impresses is the exquisite simplicity, and this makes detailed working instructions almost superfluous.

You know already how the silver wire links are passed through semi-precious stones and then bent into loops at each end. There is also nothing new about the method of stringing the coral chips together on one wire looped at both ends for joining to the other links. As well as being decorative, the wide silver ring (made by drilling a hole through the middle of a silver disc) has an important function in drawing the stones and coral chips together, thus adding to the colourful mobility of the three piece pendant.

Fig. 12. A delightful variation of the same silver necklace.

Meander-pattern brooch

What a game this was with a piece of wire — bending and spreading it into a wildly serpentine form, more like an eccentric safety-pin than a conventional brooch, yet decorative and fascinating at the same time. Because of its malleability, silver wire can be used. On the other hand, gold is just as easy to work as well as being lighter and even more brilliant in its effect.

A wire of regular width, even with the lively swirls of this design, is nothing compared to the almost throbbing irregularity of width surging along the loops of the brooch illustrated in the sketch. (Compare the same technique illustrated in the photographs on pages 84 and 85).

Use sterling silver wire (925/1000) with a thickness of about 1 mm. For spreading use a small hammer. An ordinary hammer will suffice for the time being.

The first thing is the jolly meandering into shape, which is after all the essence of this cheerful design. Of course, the sketch is only a modest attempt to get you moving on a design that grows from your own imagination and the daring twists and turns that you give to the wire.

As a first step, draw what you have in mind on a thin piece of card, and when you are satisfied, take this as the pattern of loops and bends to be followed. The operation is rather different from previous ones, however, in that, instead of bending the wire flat on the table with the drawing as a template, the sketch serves only as a guide while you shape the wire with both hands. A piece of pointed dowelling is used for forming the irregular loops.

The wire is spread by hammering it on a smooth, flat steel plate. An ordinary household hammer (about a 2-in. head with a $2\frac{1}{2}$-in. face) needs a little attention if it is to give the best results. To remove scratches, smooth with emery-paper, rough, medium and fine grades, in that order.

Use the hammer carefully, making light, even blows in the right places to control the amount of spreading. Take care also not to alter the character of the curves in the wire by an exclusive concentration on the spreading. A good precaution is to hold the two end loops together with

31

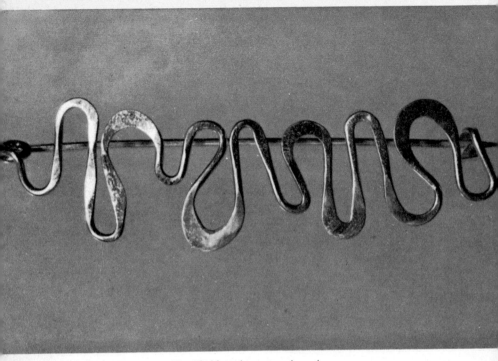

Fig. 13. Meander-pattern brooch.

binding wire so that the curves don't wander off, into an arabesque of their own.

Something that experience can turn to advantage is the tendency of the wire to curl under the hammer blows. To combine the two operations of spreading and curving in one, bend the curves at the start in a more pronounced way. Continue hammering until both the spread and the curves are satisfactory. After spreading one curve, the adjacent curve is again more tightly formed with the pliers and then flattened with the hammer in the same way. It must be emphasised, however, that such economy of effort depends on the skill and confidence that can come only with experience.

However, once the skill is learnt, it can be seen that this method is superior; the use of binding wire is now superfluous and the combined operation provides a greater control of the wire and less likelihood of distortion at any point.

Finally, the pin of the brooch must be formed and hardened. Like a large safety-pin, this has a bold double loop, formed so as to stand perpendicularly to the face of the brooch. For the pin to have enough tension, the loop is curved tightly around the smooth end of a needle file. To ensure that the pin maintains both shape and strength, it is hammered evenly, the blows being delivered in a progressive spiral towards the point. The point of the pin is filed and finally hammered once again.

The hook in which the point of the pin is secured is made by flaring the wire at the other end of the brooch and bending it over like the top of a picture-hanger. If the hammering results in a work-hardening that makes it difficult to bend the hook, then it can be lightly annealed in a light red flame, left to cool and then easily bent into shape

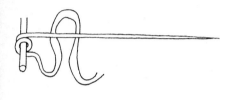

Ear-ring

This charming and amusing piece of jewellery is the result of what a critic could call a misuse of skill on a piece of gold or silver wire. For example, the fruit-like blobs that embellish the ends of the radial fingers of the ear-ring are the result of a technique learned from faulty soldering — when too much heat makes the solder "sizzle" and form blobs instead of cleanly knitting the joint.

To make the ear-ring you need 0·6 mm. thick round wire, a hollowing block, ball punches and soldering equipment.

Six pieces of wire are cut, each about 2 in. long. Later, of course, the wire will be considerably shortened by the formation of the blobs at the end. Use a pair of pointed nose pliers to bend each one of the wires in the middle, forming an angle of between thirty and forty degrees. After cleaning the points of the V-shaped wires properly, arrange all of them on a piece of asbestos in a circular fashion with the points touching in the middle. With flux, silver solder and heat we can then join them all into a twelve-pointed silver star. Apply a pointed flame just long enough to melt the ends of the twelve fingers until they seem to shrink and form a pod-like blob in a sudden flash of heat. Take care not to heat to the point where the blobs fall off. Keep it up until you are satisfied both with the length of each of the twelve spokes of the star and the size of the blobs at the end. Finally, as the bottom sketch illustrates, the star is domed carefully in the usual way. It is important, after soldering and annealing, to pickle in dilute sulphuric acid in order to remove the oxidized scale from the metal, and then to smooth with steel wool.

Finally, a clip must be attached to the domed star so that it can be worn. You can either make a clip or, better still, you can buy a ready-made one and solder it in the usual way to the inside of the star. Clean the part to be soldered, brush with flux, place a solder chip in position, apply heat, and use a pair of pliers to press the clip into place as soon as the solder runs.

Ring and cross necklace

We are also indebted to a goldsmith for the idea behind this attractive necklace. However, the original design has been somewhat simplified and adapted to the needs of the beginners who will use this book.

Silver wire with a square cross-section is cut as required and bent by hand into approximately circular shapes. These are then placed on a piece of iron rod and hammered gently into perfect ring shapes. Finally, they are flattened and spread in the usual way. Work-hardening is countered by annealing, followed by pickling. The decorative traces of the hammer blows should remain. The bold cross links are made from sheet silver about one-third the thickness of the rings (about 1mm.). They are cut to size, bent over and flattened before soldering, as shown in the sketch. However, both the rings and the cross links can remain unsoldered so long as you take care to loop and bend in such a way that the rings and crosses keep their shape and position through their own inner tension or spring.

Left unsoldered, the connecting links made out of sheet silver do not need the cross pieces. On the other hand, since they are loops hammered flatter in the middle than at the ends (as the sketch illustrates), they have enough spring to hold the cross pieces in position. However, soldering is easy, especially with steel clips to hold the work together during the soldering operation.

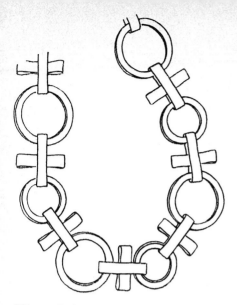

Silver chain with flat wire rings

The chain consists of twenty-four large rings (5-in. inner diameter) linked together by pairs of small rings. The two rings of each double link are not otherwise joined together. The size, wire thickness and number of rings can be varied.

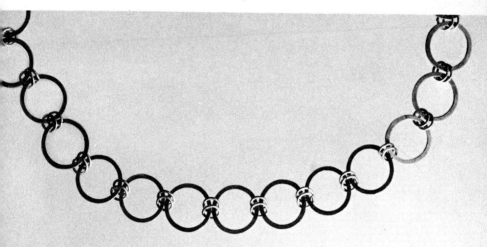

Fig. 14. Silver ring chain. Materials: square silver wire, 925/1000, 1 mm. thick, and round wire, also 925/1000, and about 0·4–0·5 mm. thick.

Long dome necklace

The pod-shaped elements in this necklace are made in exactly the same way as the domed discs illustrated in figure 11.

First of all a hollow or depression is needed as the matrix for mass-producing the metal pods. Hard wood, rather than the more expensive steel, is good enough for doming soft sheet silver; there is no need for the precision that steel gives.

First draw a sketch on paper, out of which a template is made to transfer the outline to the hard wood block. The hollow is cut out with a gouge or a sharp knife. The same template is used to mark the outlines of the pods on the sheet silver before cutting out. The flat, oval shaped pieces are then hollowed or domed by striking with a ball punch and hammer until they assume the shape of the depression in the hard wood block. Naturally each piece is annealed before hollowing. Spread the blows evenly and, once again, retain the traces of the punch blows to enhance the appearance of the surface. While smoothness is a characteristic of mass-production in the car industry for example, neverthless metalwork of this kind is at its best when it gives evidence not only of thoughtful design but also of the very processes involved in realizing that design.

During the doming operation, the pods may well be bent a little out of shape but this can be corrected by placing them, after heating, edge-downwards on a flat surface where they regain their shape under their own weight. Finally, the edges are scraped and filed to remove other irregularities.

Small double rings are necessary to attach the pods to the twin chains of the necklace. 0·4–0·5 mm. thick silver wire is looped tightly around a 2 mm. thick brass rod to form a tight spiral. Before winding the spiral, a thin layer of tissue-paper is wrapped once only around the rod. Burning the paper provides the necessary looseness for easy removal of the wire spiral. Open loops are produced in the usual way by sawing along the length of the spiral. Twin loops are then made by springing them lightly together in pairs and then soldering the open joints together in one single operation. The twin loops are soldered to the ends of the pods and threaded with the double chain (purchased from a jeweller's or craft shop).

The pods hang with their open sides facing outwards, and, on a slender throat, the effect is charming, transforming a basic and primitive design into a decorative and sophisticated piece of jewellery.

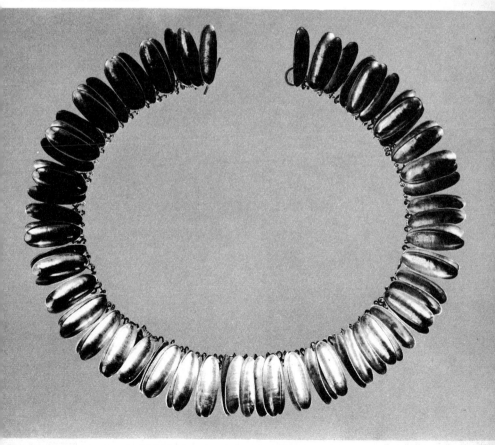

Fig. 15. Long dome necklace. Materials: two thin silver chains and 0·4 mm. thick sheet silver.

Ring with cone-shaped stone

The stone is cheap amethyst, quartz or agate, shaped and polished by a stone cutter according to a wooden model of what is required. Instead of a semi-precious stone, the cone centre-piece can be made of ebony, amber or ivory. For this project it is worth considering making a prototype in copper.

The square rod is flared, as shown in the sketch, at both ends, using the paper template as a guide. Marks of the flat faced hammer blows are removed with a file and emery-paper. The ends are then curved to the shape of the stone, as indicated in the photograph, and the sketch, lower right. This is done by laying the ring's ends over a depression in a lead sheet and then doming gently with a hammer and a ball punch.

The triangular platform is made by drilling a hole at the apex of the triangle and sawing both sides as shown in sketch. Score the base of the triangle lightly or heavily according to the thickness of metal and place the metal in a bench vice with the groove just above the jaws of the vice. First punch inwards and then punch flat from the top.

The narrow part of the metal is now curved to the required shape and size over a metal rod or ring-shaping cone with light blows from a hammer and then gently squeezed into line between the jaws of a clamp.

The bending and hammering give a certain tension to the ring. The sharp edges are rounded with a file and the whole thing is then smoothed and polished with emery-paper. The ends will, of course, be sprung closer together than the width of the stone, and in order to insert the stone into position, the ring is gently forced open by means of the conical mandrel which is removed just as gently when the stone sits firmly in place, although some play will make very little difference.

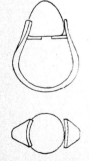

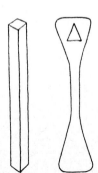

Fig. 16. Ring with cone-shaped stone.

Fig. 17. Drilled stone ring.

Drilled stone ring

Because of the way the stone is set, this ring is a little easier to make. The holes in the ends of the ring are drilled only after the ring has been bent into shape, in order to ensure that they are properly aligned. Wire to hold the stone (or wood, ivory, etc.) in position is cut to size so that the ends protrude, as shown in the photograph. At one end solder a washer and short length of tube in position, as shown in the sketch. The stone is set in place as previously described and the wire is pushed far enough through for a washer and tube to be soldered at the other end. The protruding ends of the wire are clinched with a hammer. If soldering is dispensed with, fine silver wire can be used and clinched in the same way. Fine silver (1000/1000) is softer, and the ends can be clinched more easily where they protrude beyond the short lengths of fine tubing.

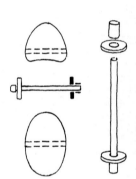

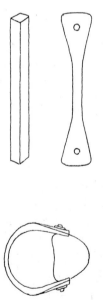

40

Gold Jewellery with Wire and Sheet

The assertion made in the first part of this book that because of its price gold can play no significant part in metal working as a hobby needs no further emphasis. However, it seems sensible to include a couple of projects in which the manner of working as well as the design give point to the simplicity and charm of this kind of gold jewellery.

Gold chain-mail necklace with pearls

The basic element in the construction of this particular necklace is once again the wire ring, linked together in such a way that the large number of small rings give the necklace a subtle kind of mobility. As the photograph shows, there are two ring-groupings; double figures-of-eight in the top part of the necklace and single figures-of-eight in the lower part where the pearls are attached. These ring-groupings are in turn linked together by rings of the same size. The pearl wires are soldered to the lower rings of the single figures-of-eight. The varying lengths of the wire are a deliberate part of the design. Its success can be seen from the flowing rhythm the irregularly suspended pearls give to the necklace.

With all the suggestions that the text and photograph provide, real success comes only as a result of your own original efforts and growing powers of discernment. Detailed instructions ensure to a certain extent avoidance of particular mistakes but, on the other hand, experience, with all the errors it may involve, is still the best teacher. There is often much greater satisfaction to be gained by departing from the original idea and following your own way instead.

For example, the appearance of the necklace might be enhanced by extending the pearls right round the chain instead of confining them only to the lower half. For practical and aesthetic considerations, the pearl wires should become progressively shorter towards the clasp.

The art of making the rings and soldering them is something already well known but there is no harm in mentioning

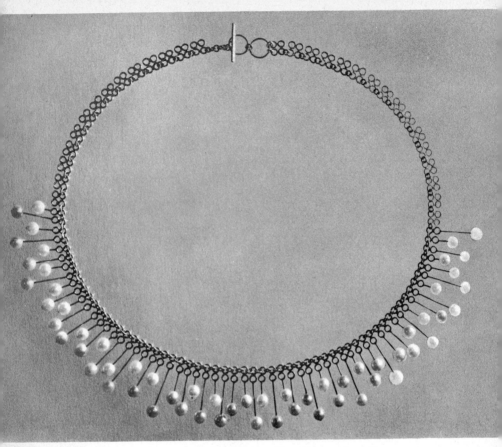

Fig. 18. Gold chain-mail necklace with pearls.

that gold solder comes in hard, medium and soft grades (the latter is best for the beginner) and that the composition of the solder should agree exactly with that of the gold wire.

The clasp is the bar and ring type shown in the photograph. By means of two fixed and two loose eyelets, the bar is attached to one end of the chain, while two large rings are attached to the other end. The double ring attachment could just as easily be a single one, the second one in this case serving only to lengthen the necklace as necessary.

The pearls still have to be fixed in place. Buy pearls with holes already bored through them, and choose the size of wire to suit the holes in the pearls. The wire is pushed through the pearls so that one end protrudes slightly. This end is flattened with light hammer blows, and it is then filed into a conical shape with the base of the cone at the end of the wire, so that it is hardly visible when the wire is drawn back through the pearl. The wire is pushed out slightly again and the hole is filled with pearl cement before drawing the wire back into position.

The cost of the necklace will be determined by the choice you make between genuine, cultured and imitation pearls.

Gold ring with pearl

The body of the ring consists of a triple arrangement of gold wire, the middle one shaped separately and the two outer ones shaped out of a continuous length of wire formed into a kind of double ring with a loop at each end, as shown in the photograph. First of all, a ring is made out of wire of the desired thickness cut to a length of about 20 in. (depending on the required size) bent into shape and then soldered. The joint is smoothed and polished before hammering exactly into shape on a sugar-loaf mandrel, with a small mallet. The length of the wire required for the loop ended double ring is calculated by doubling the circumference of the completed ring and adding 4 in. for the loops to hold the pearl in place. Twice twenty plus four gives a total

Fig. 19. Gold ring with pearl. Materials: 0·9 mm. thick round wire, gold 750/1000.

length of 44 in. The actual shaping operation can be worked out from previous experience. All it consists of is shaping the wire into a large ring, soldering the ends together, cleaning and smoothing the joint, and then folding into it a double ring with the loops at each end. The single ring is pushed into place between the coils of the double ring and all three are now carefully soldered together. The end loops are worked so that they curve outwards slightly but stand close enough to fit around the pearl. In addition, the pearl is held in place by means of a short length of wire soldered into the centre of the middle ring. This fits into a hole already drilled in the pearl and is fixed firmly in place with pearl cement. All that remains to be done is to clean the joints with a file and scraper, and then to smooth and polish.

Wire and Sheet Brass for Bigger Items

Pretzel stand

A plan is needed to begin with but, instead of sketching it with pencil and paper, it is better to fashion a kind of proto-type out of binding wire. In this way a compromise is reached between the imagination and the material, initially vague ideas can take shape as the wire is bent with the fingers. Finally, the success of the design can be assessed in terms of size, shape, stability and usefulness, and when these are satisfied, work can begin.

Soft, drawn wire, 1·8–2·0 mm. thick, is used throughout. It can be obtained from any metal supplier who deals in non-ferrous metals. Similarly he can supply the sheet brass that will be required for later projects, too.

As the photograph shows, the stand is made up of two pieces of wire. The base of the stand is fashioned from a rectangle in which the shorter sides correspond in length roughly to the vertical span of the central ellipse. In fact, they should be a little longer to allow for the upward curving of the feet.

A single piece of wire is used for shaping the rectangle, the ends being soldered where they meet, preferably with the joint located where the wire is straight or only gently curving, rather than where there is a sharp curve.

For larger joints like this, the best flux is Borax bought in cone form if possible or, failing that, as a powder. An earthenware Borax tray (a plant-pot holder, for example) is used to produce a thin Borax paste by rubbing the cone in a circular motion in a little water. A piece of porcelain can be used for mixing Borax powder and water into a milky paste.

The joint is brushed with the Borax paste and a 1 mm. long soft silver solder chip is placed in position by means of the damp brush before applying heat by the blowpipe method.

The job can be done a little more easily with a soldering-iron and tin solder. An electric soldering-iron is the most convenient, used with core solder, another delightful labour-saver since it combines in one, a casing of solder and a flux core. When using tin solder, however, the joint must be as unobtrusive as possible.

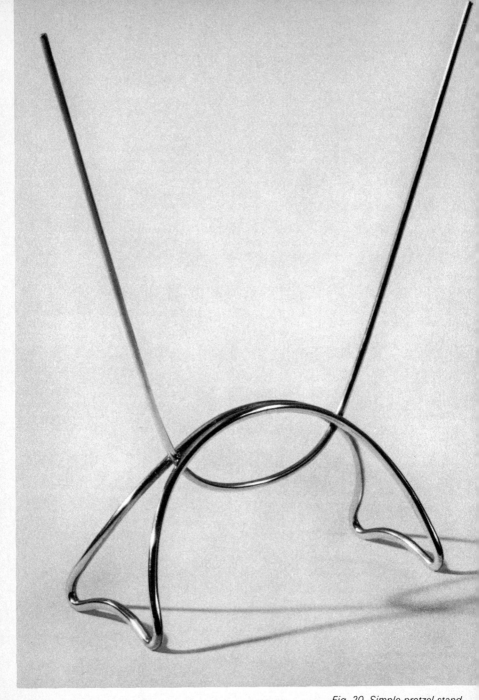

Fig. 20. Simple pretzel stand.

The next step is to make the slight curve in the short sides of the rectangle and then pinch the long sides together so that they meet, evenly curving, in the middle. They are tied together with binding wire before soldering for a distance of just under 1 in. where they touch. This is done from underneath so that the joint is invisible. After that it is curved upwards into a rounded arch to form the finished base. The actual pretzel bearer is curved into a fan-like U-shape before being pushed upwards through the base and soldered into position.

A similar stand for table napkins

In this job the only technical difficulties encountered are in the few places that need soldering, although you will by now have gained such confidence in carrying out that process that you will no longer consider it a problem. All that remains is to describe the basic shape of the stand and to explain what is involved in bending the wire.

The basic shape is a rectangle with boldly curved corners, but before getting down to work with the wire, draw the outline on card with a soft pencil, and then cut it out before bending upwards to see if the resulting curve is actually what you want. This card can be used as a template when bending the wire. The wires that make the two central arches are shaped independently of one another, except as far as the length is concerned because their ends have to be soldered together.

The rectangles are shaped and soldered in the usual way, care being taken to ensure that the end curves of both rectangles show the necessary symmetry. The next step is to form — again separately — the steep upward curves — gentler on the lower rectangle — to provide the deep saddle-shape in which the napkins will lie. The curves are formed with the help of a suitable piece of dowelling — such as a broom-handle — placed in the middle of the rectangle, and pressure is applied to the wire until the right curve is achieved.

Three more pieces will complete the stand: the central arc-ended trapezium and the two curving side pieces making the feet of the stand. The two side pieces are bent separately with the aid of a template. They too, will have to be soldered into position where they touch other parts of the stand. Any irregularity can be corrected simply by placing them side by side on a flat surface and then filing the feet, or, if necessary, (in the case of gross irregularities) snipping or sawing off the excess and finishing with a file. The vertical, inverted stirrup is also bent with the help of a template. To ensure complete regularity of the figure, it is best to cut the template out of a folded piece of paper, with the fold as the central axis of a symmetrical figure. The ends of the wire are not yet soldered together. First, it is placed vertically in position as shown in the photograph, and soldered in those places where it touches the other wires on either side of the saddle. The open end is at the top, of course, and only after soldering the sides in place is the top joint finally closed and soldered.

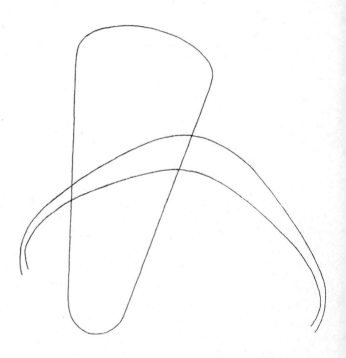

Basic shapes of the napkin stand. Half full-size.

Fig. 21. Napkin stand.

49

Another stand – wire and sheet metal

This variation of the original pretzel stand bears a close resemblance to it except that the base is made out of sheet metal and that the wire bearers are provided with large loops to keep the pretzels in position.

The sheet metal base is made in this way: first draw the sketch (on folded paper to ensure symmetry) check and amend until satisfactory, transfer to thin card, cut it out and bend into the required shape. When satisfied with the size and shape, use the card as a template to mark the outline on the sheet brass (English Standard Brass, Ms 63,1 mm. thick). Remember to mark the outline close to the edge of the brass sheet in order to waste as little as possible of the material you have bought. Saw carefully around the outline (patiently as well, to save saw blades) and then file accurately to the line, checking against the template to ensure accuracy. Finally, finish round the edges of the metal with a few light strokes of the smoothing file.

Unlike the earlier base made out of wire, this one cannot be bent with the fingers. The metal strip is bent into a bold arch by beating it out with a mallet on a previously shaped piece of wood. A steel hammer will leave marks that are difficult to remove. The holes for the bearers are drilled before bending the strip. After passing the wire through these holes the large triangular loops are shaped at right-angles to the arms, as shown in the photograph. The wire arms are fixed in place by soldering on the underside of the holes. As far as the rounded triangular loops are concerned, the tension imparted by bending makes soldering unnecessary.

A certain amount of smoothing and polishing of the arms and base should take place before soldering together. This is done progressively with various grades of emery-cloth, down to the finest. Emery files are most suitable, consisting of flat strips of wood covered with emery-paper (glued or pinned in place) which you can either make quite easily for yourself or purchase in a hardware store. First get rid of coarse blemishes and scratches, and finally smooth in one direction along the length to get the fine finish to be seen in the photograph.

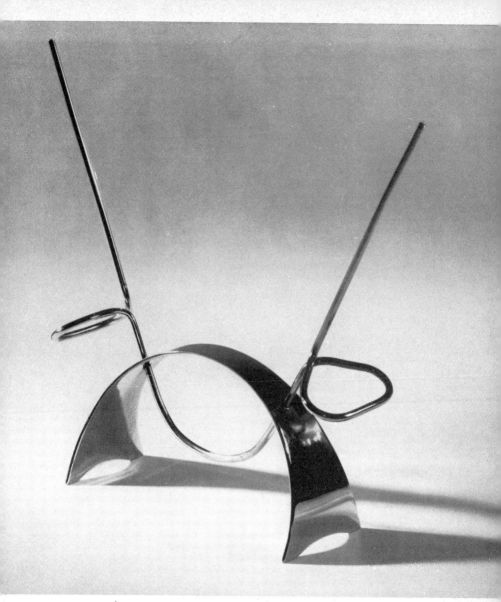

Fig. 22. Pretzel stand — wire and sheet metal.

Three or four armed candlestick

It is very rare these days for a candlestick to be used as lighting. Instead, it is now used to create an atmosphere of intimacy among friends on special occasions. Much as we may like the idea of having an old-fashioned candlestick, we should guard against directing our creative attempts towards reproducing such objects. Despite the attraction of the old-fashioned kind of candlestick, it is better to work with plain drawn wire and sheet metal to produce something which combines modern design with simplicity and charm.

Again it is essential to begin with a simple sketch. First draw a side-view of a single arm of the candlestick on a piece of paper, fold the paper to provide a longitudinal axis, reproduce the arm symmetrically on the other side and check the curves to see what alterations are necessary. As the sketch shows, the candlestick consists of three or four pairs of wire rods shaped and curved in exactly the same way.

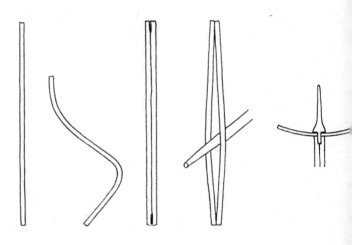

Mark out a piece of wood from the paper template as a mould for bending the arms and saw the wood a fraction on the waste side of the line smoothing finally with a rasp.

The length of wire required for each arm is measured with a piece of thread over the sketched outline. A mallet is used to beat out the required shape over the wooden template,

Fig. 23. Candlestick. Materials: brass wire 2·5 mm. thick and sheet brass, 0·7 mm. thick.

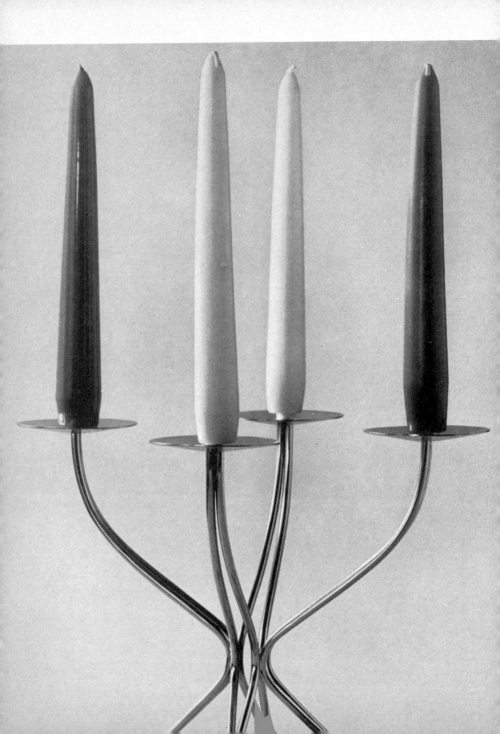

checking each wire against the drawing prepared earlier. The wires are then arranged in pairs, and held together with binding wire tied about $1\frac{1}{2}$ in. from each end. The top and bottom of each pair are soldered about $\frac{1}{2}$ in. from the ends, after which they are sawn and filed so that the ends correspond exactly. Before proceeding further, the binding wire is removed.

With a wooden rod and a little firm pressure from the fingers, the pairs of wires can now be widened in the middle, as the sketches and photograph show.

Now all that remains is to join the three or four arms together as shown in the photograph. Binding wire is used to hold them in position, first tied around the middle where they touch and then at points above and below to provide the necessary stability while fixing. Then (with soldering-iron, tin solder, zinc chloride or patented flux) the joints are carefully soldered, using very little solder in each case so that there are no unsightly lumps.

Next the drip pans. To ensure that they are in proportion to the arms, make discs out of paper and try them in position first. Use them later as templates to mark the outline on the sheet metal, before sawing out and filing carefully to the required shape, and finally rounding all the edges very slightly. As the photograph shows, the drip pans are best slightly hollowed in the middle.

This is by no means difficult and the operation has already been described in some detail. However, if you wish, the drip pans can simply be left flat.

The spikes which are used to hold the candles in place, are made from brass wire, $4–4\frac{1}{2}$ mm. in diameter. For easier working instead of sawing off each piece from the length of wire and then filing, do it in reverse — first file conically into an even spike and only then saw off the required length. Otherwise it is extremely difficult to hold the short pieces of wire with the fingers while filing.

The following method is the easiest for joining together the spike, drip pan and arm. The drip pan is placed upside down on a suitably shaped piece of crosscut timber, and struck exactly in the middle with a centre punch to produce an indentation into which the end of the double-wired arm will fit. The indentation on the base of the drip pan is, of course, a raised boss on the other side.

All pieces are prepared for soldering in the usual way. The drip pan is laid face-downwards on the bench, the arm of the candlestick is fixed in position and soldered. If the drip pans do not sit properly on the arms, then they can always be removed and re-soldered.

Fig. 24. Four armed candlestick.

The most difficult part of the whole operation is the last one — ensuring that the spikes are upright and dead-centre in the middle of the drip pans before soldering into position.

The raised boss referred to above makes it easier to produce a tidy joint. It can fit into a shallow hole drilled in the relatively broad base of the spike. The spike is held upside down in the bench vice, and drilled with a bit approximating as closely as possible to the size of the disc's punched boss.

Lightly tin the inside of the drilled hole in the base of the spike, using the blowpipe rather than the soldering-iron. Then, rest the spike on the raised boss in the middle of the disc before heating it from base to tip with the soldering-iron for the solder to take. Remember to clean the soldering-iron thoroughly before doing this in order to avoid having unsightly solder smears on the spike. The spike itself will be too hot to handle, and for that reason a piece of wood can be used to press it firmly into position.

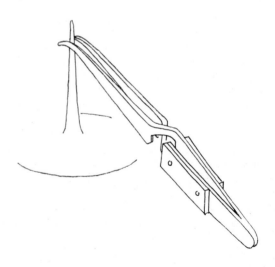

Using the hawkbill tongs to hold the spike while soldering.

Paper-knife from sheet metal — sawn and filed

If you have by now had enough of hammering and soldering and you want to immerse yourself in filing for a while, here is a simple little project involving filing a piece of sheet brass ($\frac{1}{8}$ in. (3 mm.) thick, about $8\frac{1}{4}$ in. long and $\frac{5}{8}$ in. wide) into a slim, tapering paper-knife.

Whatever shape you choose, the one illustrated in the sketch or one of your own design, the first step is to draw the outline in the usual way. Transfer it to the sheet brass and carefully saw around the outline.

In addition to being a test of skill it is also a test of patience — working time, depending on proficiency, will occupy two or three hours.

Using the working drawing as a template, the rough saw lines are accurately finished with a file. The next step, which will certainly provide you with some considerable insight into the art of filing, is to taper the metal from its 3 mm. thick handle to a fine pointed tip at the end of the roughly 1 mm. thick blade. After gently sharpening the blade, the edges and corners of the handle are lightly rounded to make it comfortable for handling.

Use pumice-stone and water to smooth and polish the faces and edges of the paper-knife, taking care, as explained in the introduction, to finish by smoothing in one direction. To prevent tarnishing, the paper-knife is covered with a light film of Japan lacquer applied with a small fixative spray.

Fondue fork

The undoubted social appeal of this Swiss savoury accounts for its growing popularity. But even as one enjoys the conversation and company gathered around the fondue, one would like to enjoy the contents with one's own fork. Cap the forks with a variety of colourful balls for easy identification. It is relatively easy to mass-produce a set of forks to cater for the largest company likely to be invited to enjoy such a dish.

A number of 10 in. steel wire lengths are cut with a saw or tin-snips. One end will carry the coloured wooden ball while the other will be worked into a pair of suitably shaped prongs. For this, one end of the wire must be spread for about 1$\frac{3}{4}$ in. from the end, as illustrated in the photograph. It is first heated in charcoal to a cherry red colour, and then spread with a few powerful hammer blows. Speed is essential since spreading can be done only as long as the metal retains its redness, and frequent re-heating is to be avoided.

When all the wire pieces have been spread in this way, the next step is to mark out the prongs and to saw out the narrow V between them with a tough, coarse saw blade. If the steel proves too hard for sawing, it will have to be annealed by heating to a cherry red colour before leaving it to cool slowly, insulated from the air in a bed of warm ash. The prongs will now be easier to saw and finish with a file and emery-cloth.

Setting the wooden ball in position is simple: a hole is drilled in the middle, using a bit the same diameter as that of the steel wire. The wooden ball is dipped in water to make it swell before fitting it on the end of the wire, tapping it lightly with a hammer if necessary. If this is carefully done, there will be no need to secure the ball to the wire with adhesive or extra fixing attachments.

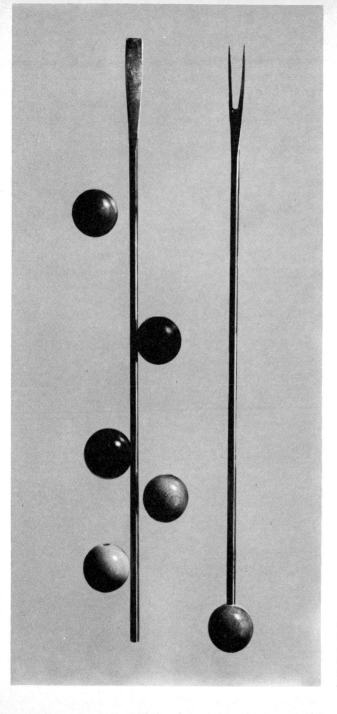

Fig. 25. Fondue fork.
Materials: bright drawn
steel wire, 3·5–4 mm. in
diameter, and coloured
wooden balls, 18–20 mm.
in diameter.

Container for cigarettes, tea or coffee

Soldering the joints is the most difficult thing in making a round box, and the beginner will need to prepare very carefully if he is to carry out the operation successfully. For this reason the soldered joint is located along the pointed leading edge of the box as illustrated in the diagrams and the photograph, so that it is accessible for filing and finishing.

The first step is to make accurate working drawings of the four parts of the box as illustrated on this page and opposite. Since they will serve as templates for marking the outlines on the sheet metal, they are drawn full size, with the aid of drawing-board, T-square and set-square, if possible. In the case of the rim and sides of the box, draw a base line with vertical lines at regular intervals as shown in the sketches. Remember that your drawing is full-size while the drawings on these two pages are half-scale. To transfer the shape of the rim of your drawing, first draw a base line to touch the lower curve of the sketch provided. Then measure the distance from the base line to the curved line along the vertical guide-lines. Double, and transfer to the working drawing, eventually joining all the dots together in a smoothly flowing curve. The same method is used in drawing the sides of the box. In the case of the base and top, however, a vertical line is drawn centrally through the points, and a series of horizontal guide-lines are added at regular intervals for a similar accurate transfer of the outline to the full-size working drawings.

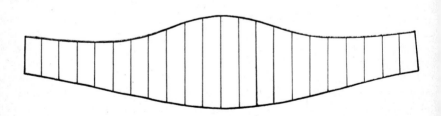

Shape of the deep outer rim of the box in fig. 26. Scale: half full-size.

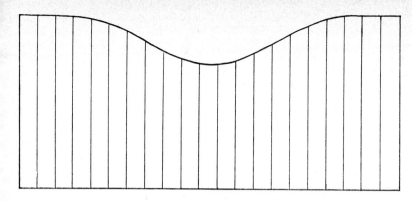

Shape of the body of the box illustrated overleaf. Also half full-size.

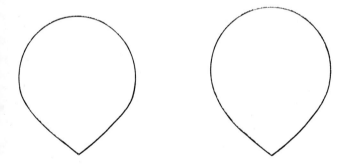

Box base (left) and lid (right). Same scale.

The photograph (Fig. 26.) shows the elegance and usefulness of the design. The tapering, low-cut front of the box makes it easy to take a cigarette from it. As a tea-caddy, on the other hand, its pointed lip makes it easy to measure out the required amount. In addition, the deep rim of the lid ensures a sufficiently tight fit to keep the contents fresh.

Fig. 26. Cigarette, tea or coffee container. Materials: standard
brass, 0·5–0·6 mm. thick sheet.

Salad-servers

The photograph opposite illustrates a pair of elegant
salad-servers. The design is such that careful consideration
must be given to the type of metal to be used in making them.
Both stainless steel and silver present certain problems: the
former because of its hardness and the latter because of its
softness. It is difficult to draw down a piece of stainless
steel from 2 mm. (the thickness of the handle) to 1 mm.
(the thickness of the "bowl"). On the other hand, while
silver is easy to draw down, its relative softness makes it
necessary to provide a much thicker handle.

Fig. 27. Tapering handles
drawn down from a 2 mm.
bar of sheet brass or silver.
Bowls of servers spread to
a thickness of 0·8 mm.
Prongs sawn out and
edges filed clean.

Sheet brass can be used and later silver plated. First draw the outline of the server on thick drawing paper or light card, cut out carefully and use as a template to transfer the outline to 2½ mm. thick piece of sheet brass. Saw and file to the line. In order not to waste any metal and also in order to avoid unnecessary effort, bear in mind that the bowl of the server will spread to twice its original width as it is drawn down. The finished thickness of the bowl is 0·8 mm. Check the outline of the bowl with the card or paper template, saw or cut once again to the line, and finish accurately with the file. The bowl is then lightly and evenly domed before bending it to incline slightly towards the handle.

The shape of the bowl can be varied, or course, and the prongs can be styled differently as well. And although the photograph illustrates servers that are 10 in. long, the length can also be changed.

63

Coat rack and umbrella stand

A hat and coat rack can be made out of various materials in a variety of different shapes. One possibility is to make a number of hanging pegs out of thick strips of aluminium and to fix them at intervals along the length of aluminium bar or tube. The sketch at the bottom of the page shows an alternative method.

However, the beginner's modest home workshop, with its emphasis mainly on cold working, is no longer adequate for projects of this kind since the frames of the umbrella stand, illustrated on the opposite page, and the hat and coat rack, illustrated below, are bent from 8–10 mm. rod in a red-hot state, and the joints must be welded.

Such a project can be undertaken only with a good forge and a proper bench vice, and for this reason you will have to seek the co-operation of a blacksmith or of an educational institution. With the right equipment, the task is comparatively simple.

The sketches indicate the nature of the work involved. 10 mm. reinforcing steel (wrought-iron rod) is used for the frame which is about 30 in. wide. To calculate the length of rod required, the whole thing is fashioned in soft aluminium wire first. This can serve as a template when bending the curves into shape. After heating the part of the metal to be bent in the blacksmith's hearth, the rod is placed in the bench vice and bent to the required shape, using the aluminium mock-up of the frame as a template. Bending should be planned to allow for the ends to be welded together at the back of the frame. Welding must be done by the professional craftsman with his special equipment.

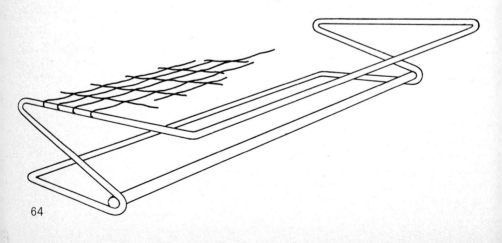

The lower acute-angled curves are drilled to take the countersunk screws holding the thick wooden rod in position. The frame can be painted in any colour with a good quality lacquer and the wooden rod left as natural. Instead of the net across the top of the frame, as indicated in the sketch, a number of nylon threads may be stretched across lengthwise.

The steel rod frame of the umbrella stand is bent in exactly the same way. It is somewhat easier because a thinner rod can be used. The base may be provided with a plastic sheet of laminate or plastic, carefully cut to size and squeezed tightly into position. Though fairly easy to fix into place, it is unlikely to provide the water-tight fit necessary on the base of an umbrella-stand. At the same time, it is consoling to think that wet umbrellas are rarely, if ever, placed in an umbrella stand.

If, on the other hand, a water-tight base is desired, then enlist the help of a skilled welder.

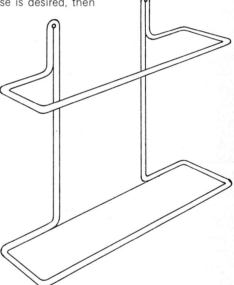

Hall-light with variations

It should be understood once again that, while the sketches on this page may be followed exactly in making the hall-light, they are intended only as guide lines, and can be varied.

The cylindrical lamp casing can be chosen from a range of thin, transparent sheet plastics. Accurately cut to match the size of the metal base ring, sheet plastic can be easily bent into a cylindrical shape and, with the joint at the back, it will keep its position under its own tension, although a second ring may be necessary at the top of the cylinder. If a ready made plastic tube is used, it is likely to slip unless it is lightly grooved where the ring grips it. The groove is best cut with a small, round file.

The fact that such a lamp will weigh no more than 2 oz. means that the brass tube (with a ninety-degree bend) that supports the bulb socket need only be soldered to the lower

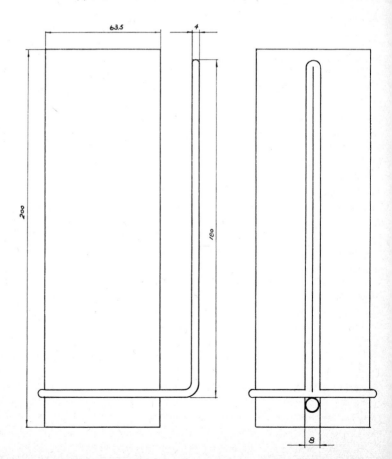

part of the double wire bracket outside the cylinder. However, the brass tubing must protrude outside the plastic cylinder a little more than the diagram (lower left) indicates.

The vertical double wire section of the bracket may be dispensed with completely. Instead, a strong brass disc may be used for attaching the lamp to the wall. In this case, a hole is drilled in the middle of the disc to fit the brass tube that supports the lamp socket. They are then soldered carefully together.

Although the sketches show that the ring and upright part of the bracket are made from a single piece of wire, it may be easier to make each piece separately and then to solder them together.

There are other possibilities, too. Instead of the wire ring at the base of the plastic cylinder, it is possible to use a strip of sheet brass fashioned into a circular clamp. Similarly the vertical double wire may be replaced by a narrow strip of sheet brass.

These suggestions should be enough to indicate the wide range of possibilities that exist in both materials and design.

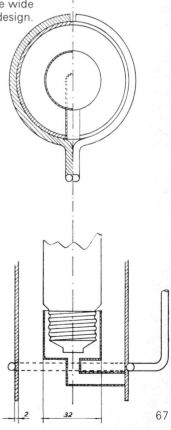

Hall-light with sheet brass reflector

The reflector consists of a square piece of sheet brass bent forward slightly at the top and the bottom, as shown in the diagram. You can, with the aid of full-size sketches, determine exactly what size you want the reflector to be. To be most effective, the reflector must be ground or polished and finally given a coat of Japan lacquer to prevent tarnishing.

A disc (or square) of Plexiglass in front of the bulb serves not only to protect the bulb but also to spread a softer light. The diameter of the disc should be the same size as the side of the square reflector.

The third element in the lamp unit consists of a single piece of brass wire bent to shape, as shown in the diagrams on the opposite page. The horizontal arms are drilled for screwing into the reflector, as shown in the diagram. Similarly the ends are drilled so that the Plexiglass disc can be attached to them with screws as shown. The lower double wire section of the bracket is bent forward as shown in the diagram and then looped at the front to take the bulb socket.

Although the diagrams show brass wire 4 mm. thick, the beginner will find it easier to work with 8–10 mm. wire

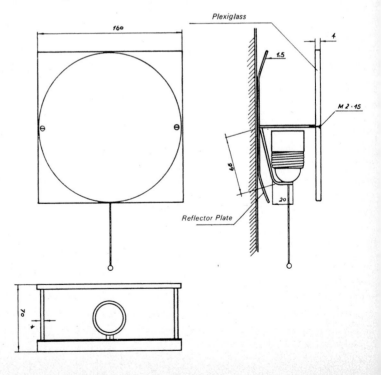

Plexiglass

Reflector Plate

when he has to drill holes and cut threads in it. It is difficult to drill holes in the ends of the wire to take the two counter-sunk screws holding the Plexiglass in position, and it will be easier to cut a thread on the ends of wire. Then solder a small washer at the end of the thread, and screw the Plexi-glass (previously bored) into position with flat or half round nuts. An even simpler way it to drill two holes near the end of each wire arm big enough and just far enough apart for split-pins to hold the Plexiglass disc firmly in position. At the same time, the distance between the bracket arms need not be the same as the diameter of the Plexiglass disc, as indicated by the position of the screws in the diagram on the opposite page. The distance between them can be shortened to bring the screws closer to the centre, if it is felt that this will improve the appearance of the lamp.

The size and shape of the loop for the bulb socket will depend on the socket, of course. The main thing is to ensure that it is firmly held in position, by the addition of a suitable cup attachment soldered into place.

Another simplification is to solder rather than screw the wire arms of the bracket to the reflector plate. This can be done with soft tin solder and a soldering iron. First of all, of course, the wire has to be cleaned and slightly flattened by filing lightly along the back of the wire.

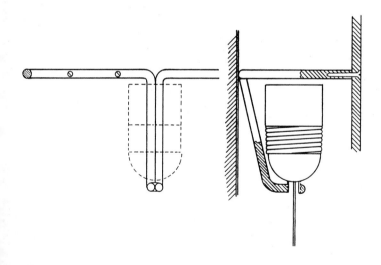

Hollowing and Raising

Raising is the traditional method of making hollow articles, which are too deep to be made on the hollowing block. The sheet-metal is worked cold, although annealing will have to take place at various stages in the process. Figure 29 on the opposite page illustrates four stages in the raising process.

The raising process stretches the metal by about 25–35 per cent, the actual amount varying from person to person of course. A good rule of thumb method of calculating the size of the sheet-metal disc required for making the bowls illustrated on pages 78 and 79, for example, is to measure the sketch from the centre of the base of the article to the lip or rim and to take that as the radius of the disc to be cut from soft sheet-metal. Most articles will be raised from sheet-metal discs about 0·6–0·8 mm. thick.

A beech wood log is fluted directly under the hammer, as shown in figure 28, and set at the right height in the bench vice. The raising hammer shown in the photograph and illustrated by the lowest of the three hammer head sketches on page 73, is used to form the radial folds simply by hammering the metal disc evenly over the groove in the log. Alternatively, this part of the raising process can be preceded by hollowing the disc on a doming block.

The right-hand photograph in figure 28 on the opposite page illustrates how the radial folds are flattened. The photograph shows the article being worked on a steel bick iron (illustrated by the sketch, lower right, page 73) but it is possible to use a suitably shaped piece of hardwood instead.

Figure 29 shows four stages in the raising process:

1. The one on the left shows traces of the first two hammering operations: the rim retains the radial folds resulting from hammering on a grooved log of wood, as shown in the top left-hand photograph of figure 28 above. After annealing and pickling, the second raising operation consists of flattening the folds by hammering outwards from the centre towards the rim. Each raising results in a relative decrease in the diameter of the metal disc and a corresponding increase in the height of the sides of the bowl – hence the term "raising".

2. The second from the left illustrates clearly how far the "raising" process has progressed. Again, it illustrates the

Fig. 28. Radial folding . . .   and flattening.

Fig. 29. Successive stages in the raising operation.

combination of radial folding and subsequent flattening of the folds from the centre. The folding-flattening process continues until the bowl reaches an approximation of the required shape. Annealing and pickling are essential after each operation, of course.

3. The third from the left illustrates an advance stage in the raising process, with the article barely showing traces of the folds around the rim. Its matt dull surface is a result of its being photographed immediately after annealing and pickling.

4. The right-hand one illustrates the bowl in its finished state. With the aid of a metal template, a planishing hammer (the top sketch on page 73) has been used to remove all dents and ridges from the surface of the bowl. This is a difficult operation, and the beginner may well find it boring and frustrating because of his inability to produce a perfect surface. In that case, it may be better to discontinue planishing at the point where the marks of the hammer may be regarded as part of the decorative design of the bowl.

The middle sketch at the top of the opposite page shows the head of a hollowing hammer used to produce a bowl shape by hammering a disc on a doming block instead of using the folding-flattening, raising method.

There are skilful silversmiths who can hollow a small dish from a small coin, hollowing it with centrally placed hammer blows until it takes on the shape of the mould in the wooden hollowing block, finally emerging as a small salt-cruet, for example, still bearing the imprint of the coin around the rim. This is illegal in the U.K!

The stakes illustrated below are, on the left, a bottoming stake for flattening the base of a vase or bowl which will have become convex during the raising or hollowing process, and, on the right, a bick iron on which the planishing of cups and vases can take place. The roughly conical bases of the stakes can be fitted into suitably shaped holes cut out of a hardwood block. The block should be high enough to allow one to work comfortably in a sitting position.

Shallow dishes, like those illustrated in figures 30 and 31, are best shaped by hammering over a rounded piece of wood, with the final planishing being done on a suitably shaped, well polished planishing stake.

If, however, the beginner's main interest is in the decorative process (chasing, embossing, repoussé), he may prefer to buy ready-made dishes or have them made to specification by a craftsman. On the other hand, the basic creative processes should not be avoided, especially since experience soon shows that the so-called technical difficulties are relatively insignificant. It does not take long to advance from the first faltering steps of the beginner to the growing skill and confidence of the budding craftsman. The

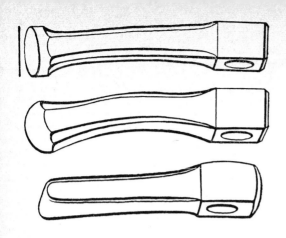

mistakes and misfortunes accompanying the beginner's efforts will themselves be regarded as an opportunity for further progress, especially if he makes them the occasion for a personal enquiry to an experienced craftsman. An introductory book, however comprehensive it tries to be, cannot mention all the obstacles the beginner is likely to meet. In this context, a learned treatise is no match for a few words dealing specifically with particular difficulties that have arisen.

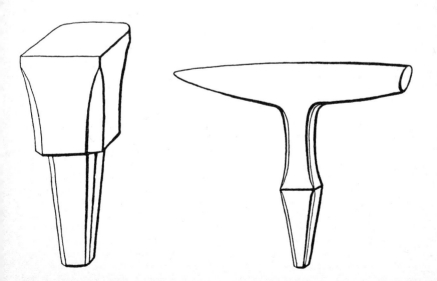

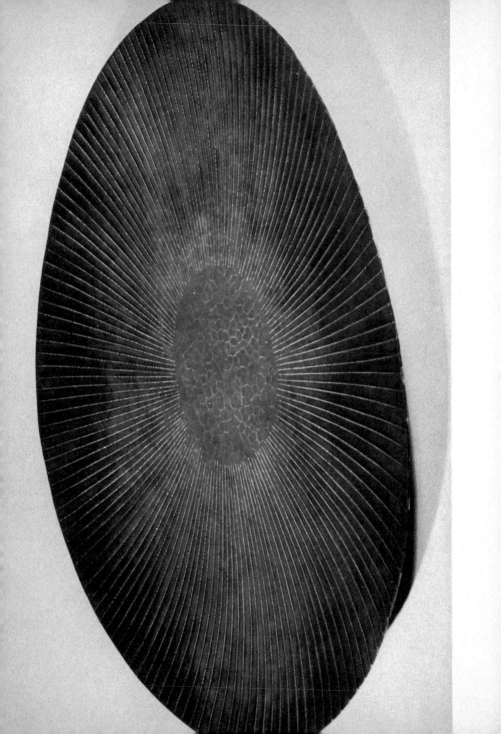

Decorative Processes

Punching and inscribing

As well as punches made out of steel, wooden punches are also available. Wooden punches are made from a hardwood such as boxwood, for example, and used to produce bold patterns on thin sheet metal over a soft under-layer. Steel punches come in a great variety of shapes (some of which are shown in the sketches) and, used with a chasing hammer, they can produce interesting patterns. An example of embossing may be seen in figure 32 in which the series of raised dots on the outside of the bowl are a result of the punch being applied to the inside of the bowl. In this case, a pearling punch (the right hand one in the sketch) was used to emboss the pattern, with the bowl placed on a suitably soft surface, such as a lead sheet or a wooden block coated with pitch. Examples of patterns produced by chasing may be seen in figures 30, 31 and 33. In the case of the bowl shown in figure 33, the wavy line pattern was chased from the outside after filling the bowl with pitch. In such cases, a metal bar is placed in the centre of the pitch to facilitate holding in the vice.

A variety of punches will be needed and these are best made out of steel bar by the beginner. Mild tool steel is best, square in cross-section and cut into 4 in. lengths, varying in thickness from 4, 5, 8 to 16 mm. The steel is filed to shape — the top tapers slightly and is left flat to take the hammer blows. The bottom part of the punch also tapers and the tip is shaped according to the pattern for which it is needed. The punches illustrated on this page are, from left to right, a straight tracing punch, a chasing punch, and a pearling punch.

It is not necessary to describe in detail how they are made. The tool steel bars are held in the vice while shaping the top and business end with the file (proceeding from rough to smooth in the usual way). Again with the file, the sharp edges are bevelled as indicated in the sketch opposite. After filing to shape, the tip of the business end of the punch is finally smoothed with emery-paper.

In the same way, the edges and corners of the punch

Fig. 30. Beaten brass dish, with embossed pattern.

stock are rounded so that no damage will be done to the surface of the metal being worked. It must be remembered that a punch is not a cutting tool like a chisel but a relatively blunt tipped instrument intended to inscribe a pattern on the surface of the metal without tearing or cutting. For this reason, the tip, too, must be finished in such a way that no part of it is likely to cut or tear.

Only the business end of the punch is hardened, for about $1\frac{1}{2}$–2 in. from the tip. With a blow torch or in a charcoal fire, it is heated until cherry red in colour (about 800 degrees centigrade) and immediately (with a pair of tongs) plunged upright into a container of cold water. To ensure rapid cooling, it must be moved about in the water to break the insulation of the steam blanket that will otherwise form around it. In this way, it will become glass hard. The hardness test is satisfied if the file no longer grips the business end of the tool but slides off instead. Only the tip of the tool is hardened in this way, the rest being left soft because of the hammer blows it will receive.

Hardened in the way described above, the tip is too brittle for use. For this reason, its hardness is reduced slightly by tempering, that is heating to about 220 degrees centigrade. The lower half of the tool is heated over an open flame. The temperatures can be judged from the colour of the oxide that forms on the surface of the steel during heating: bright yellow to pale straw = 220°C; dark straw = 240°C; yellow brown = 250°C; violet = 280°C; light blue = 310°C, and so on. We are concerned with the lowest temperature, and as soon as the yellow or pale straw tint reaches the tip, the tool is immediately quenched in cold water. The test this time is two-fold: the yellow tint must be visible when the tool is cold, and the file must grip lightly rather than slide off.

The best kind of hammer for chasing and embossing is what is known as a repoussé (or chasing) hammer, that is a hammer head with a flat, round face at one end and a ball-pin at the other end. The long, slim wooden handle culminates in a knob, rather like an Indian club. If such a hammer is unobtainable, then an ordinary hammer will do. Indeed, the ancient Egyptians made do with stones instead of hammers to punch their exquisite gold and silver reliefs.

In addition to the way the punch is lightly and consistently hammered, the position of the punch between the fingers of the left hand is also important to the success of chasing work. The even regularity of the wavy lines chased on the surface of the bowl shown in figure 33 is a result of holding the punch almost vertical but inclined slightly away from the direction of travel. The top of the punch is held between

Fig. 31. Dish with chased pattern.

forefinger and thumb, with the middle finger almost at the bottom pushing the tip of the punch against the nail of the ring finger. Under the rhythmical blows of the hammer, the punch then glides forward to produce a continuous groove rather than a disjointed series of punch marks.

Small work is set in pitch, larger work on a sand-bag, face-side down for embossing, but with the pitch or sand on the inside for chasing work. (The recipe for pitch is on page 11.) To ensure close contact between the metal and the pitch, a thin coating of the pitch is spread over the warm surface of the metal before laying the object on a pitch coated wooden block or embedding it in a tray or bowl of pitch.

A cold pitch under-layer has the effect of hardening the outlines of the pattern, while warm pitch tends to soften the outline of the punched dots, dashes and lines of the pattern.

Fig. 32. Pattern embossed with pearl punch.

Instead of pitch or a sand-bag, the beginner can use a thick sheet of lead to support the face of the object to be embossed. Before getting down to work with hammer, punches and sheet metal, the beginner will find it easier to practise all that is involved by doing the same kind of decoration on aluminium foil with the aid of wooden modelling tools.

The decision to chase or emboss is entirely a matter of personal preference, having regard both to the pattern and the surface to be decorated. In the case of the shield-like, shallow dish (fig. 30) with its raised curved lines radiating from the centre, embossing seemed most appropriate. For the deep bowl (fig. 33), chasing seemed to be both the most practical and attractive way of inscribing the smooth, wavy line pattern.

Fig. 33. Pattern chased with tracing punch.

Ancient and modern American jewellery

A careful examination of some of the oldest South American ornaments side by side with the works of an artist active in the United States of America in modern times, reveals interesting points of comparison in form and technique as well as intriguing contrasts in style.

The golden armlet (fig. 34) dates from the Inca period in Peru while the other pieces of jewellery are the work of Alexander Calder whose fame has spread throughout the world as a result of his artistic mobiles which Jean Paul Sartre described as ". . . strange forms made up of stalks, palm-branches, discs, feathers and petals". Jewellery (if this term may be applied to the strangely shaped creations) occupied only a small part of his time. It is, however the element of fun that emerges as the most powerful characteristic of his work, whether it is a piece of jewellery or one of his "Stabiles". It is not strictly true to say that, in contrast to the Incas, Calder avoided the kind of joint that required the application of heat, although his preference was for cold working, wire bending and simple methods of joining pieces together. He was not averse occasionally, as the photographs

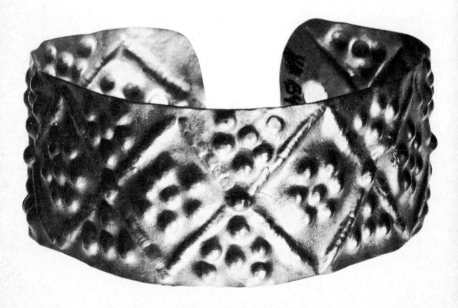

Fig. 34. Golden armlet from Peru. Embossed diamond rosette pattern. The rather blurred pattern is the result of embossing over a soft under-layer of sand or warm pitch.

show, to the use of rivets for attaching one piece to another. Calder's work exhibits indeed a self-conscious preference for the technically simple and primitive.

What is the undeniable strength of his work? And why does this book include photographs of pieces of jewellery that appear (at first sight at least) to include very little of any technical interest?

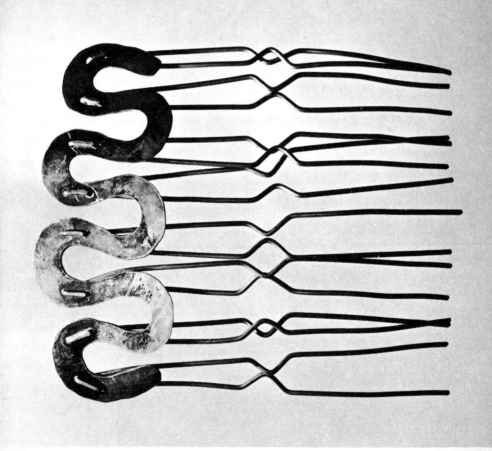

Fig. 35. Ornamental comb from round, flat-beaten silver wire. Typical of Calder's work, the round-wire teeth are not soldered in place but pushed through holes drilled in the beaten silver and then hammered firmly into position. The work is done cold.

It must be emphasized that the reader is not expected to copy these pieces of jewellery. On the contrary, they are intended to stimulate the reader to create his own original forms, with an emphasis on the elementary and primitive not only in technique but in form as well. Technical progress will increase as the beginner recognizes that, when hammered flat and bent in its cold state, wire is likely to assume the most extravagant shapes. Effective design can well result from following the patterns to be found in nature, as in the wave like curves of the comb (fig. 35), the strange insect (fig. 36), or the reed drawn hieroglyphs (fig. 39).

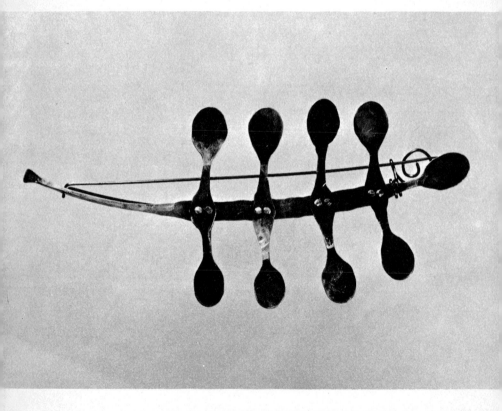

Fig. 36. Another unconventional brooch by Calder, impressive in size and intriguing in shape. Typical, too, is the manner of joining the arms to the main stem of the brooch – riveted rather than soldered. Fig. 38. shows how close, central spirals may be drawn out and flattened into a variety of boomerang shapes.

Fig. 37. Silver necklace emphasizing once again the basically
primitive style and technique of the artist. Thick wire is beaten flat
and bent into a variety of lancet shapes. They are strung together
without further treatment. In this case the apparent lack of
proportion is striking.

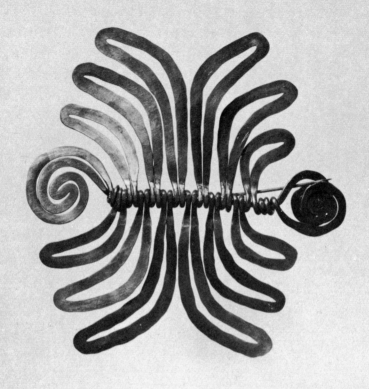

Fig. 38. Again flat beaten wire drawn into a pattern that appears to have been drawn with a loosely flowing, broad nibbed pen.

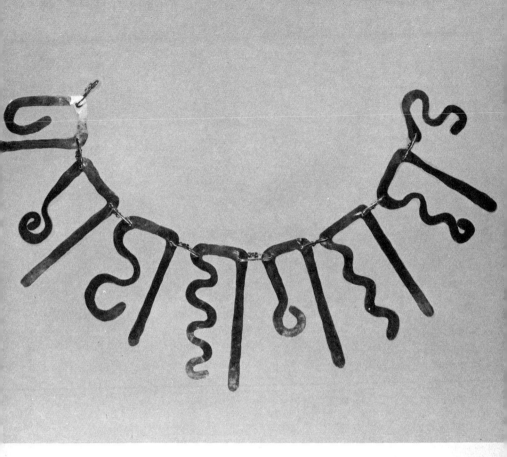

Fig. 39. Another of Calder's primitive necklaces, each piece being
drawn into a slender, slightly undulating leaf shape, on which the
traces of the hammer blows can clearly be seen through a
magnifying glass.

Rifflers

In addition to wooden handled rasps and files, there is also a wide range of small curved files, usually double-ended, used in chasing and smoothing intricate work. They are known as rifflers and may be purchased from good tool suppliers.

The sketches below illustrate the basic shapes and sections: from left to right, flat, three square, four square, round and ball.

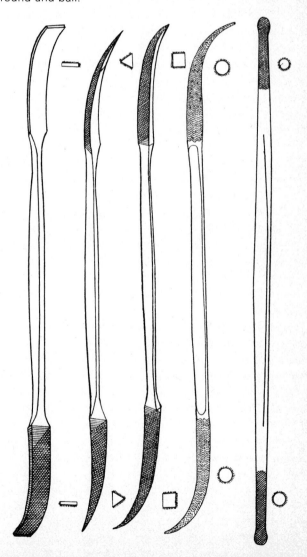

These sketches are about three-quarters of the actual size.

Needle or Swiss files

Unlike the curved rifflers, these files are straight but they are available in the same variety of sectional forms. They are intended for fine work and must be treated with great care as they snap very easily. If necessary, they can be easily converted into rifflers by heating to a cherry red colour, quickly bending to shape over a piece of wood, heating once again to a glowing red heat, and quenching as already described elsewhere. Tempering is unnecessary, and the files remain glass hard.

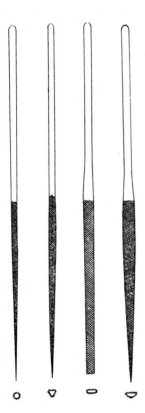

Also about three-quarters of the actual size.

Index

Calder, Alexander 80–1

Carat 7

Cement 43–4

Chemicals
potassium sulphide 9
Schlipper's salt 9
sodium sulphide 9
sulphuric acid 10, 11, 34
zinc chloride 55

Finish
colouring 9, 17, 65
lacquer 65
japan 8, 57, 68
patina 8, 9
polishing 10, 38, 43, 44, 50, 57

Flux 10, 17, 34, 45, 55
Borax 10, 17, 45

Form 18–19, 28, 82

Materials
agate 30, 38
alloys 8, 9, 11, 23, 31
aluminium 11, 17, 64
amber 38
amethyst 21, 38
beads 18, 21
brass 8, 9, 11, 17, 23, 50, 55, 57, 63, 66–7, 68
copper 8, 11, 17, 38
coral 30
gold 7, 31, 33, 41, 42–3
ivory 38, 40
lead 21, 38, 79
pearls 41–4
plastic 65, 66
plexiglass 68, 69
quartz 38
clear 30
rose 21, 29
smoky 21
silver 8, 11, 12, 15, 21, 23, 29, 30, 31, 33, 34, 36, 40, 60, 63
solder 17, 34, 56
gold 42
silver 8, 10, 45
tin 10, 55, 69

steel 21, 34, 65, 75
reinforcing 64
stainless 62
wire 24, 58
wood 21, 36, 40, 52, 70, 72, 75
ebony 38

Oxidation 8, 10, 17, 34, 77

Processes
annealing 8, 10, 33, 34, 36, 58, 70–2
chasing 11, 72, 75, 77–9, 86
doming 21, 29, 34, 36, 38, 63, 70, 72
drilling 24, 38, 40, 56, 65, 68
embossing 11, 72, 75, 78–9
filing 24, 38, 42, 44, 48, 50, 55, 57, 58, 63, 69, 75
hammering 31–2, 33, 36, 40, 42, 43, 58, 70, 72, 78, 82
heating 8, 24, 58, 77, 87
link making 14, 17–18, 22, 24, 26, 29, 30, 32–3, 34, 36
pickling 8, 10–11, 34, 70–2
planishing 72
punching 36, 38, 55
raising 70–2
repoussé 11, 72
riveting 8
sawing 17, 26, 38. 50, 55, 57, 58, 63
soldering 10, 15, 17–19, 21, 26, 33–4, 36, 40, 44, 45, 47, 48, 50, 55–6, 66–7, 69
tempering 77
welding 64, 65

Templates 12, 23, 31, 38, 47, 48, 50, 52, 55, 57, 60, 63, 64

Tools
anvil 5, 12
bick iron 70
blow-pipe 56
emery-cloth and paper 10, 31, 38, 50, 58, 75
files 5, 12, 44, 50, 86–7
hammers 5, 12, 31, 38, 72, 75, 79
mallet 12, 44, 50, 52
mandrel 38, 43
pitch block 11, 78
punches 5, 21, 38, 75–8, 79
repoussé 77
sandbag 78
saws 5
scraper 44
soldering iron 12, 45, 55, 56, 60, 69
stakes 12, 72
vice 5, 38, 64, 75